TENTS IN THE CLOUDS

TENTS IN
THE CLOUDS

*The First Women's Himalayan
Expedition*

BY
MONICA JACKSON AND
ELIZABETH STARK

Foreword by Arlene Blum

SEAL PRESS

Cover design: Clare Conrad
Cover photos: Front cover (foreground) by Roger Mear/Tony Stone Images. Front and back cover (background) by Elizabeth Stark. Photos of Monica Jackson, Elizabeth Stark and Evelyn Camrass courtesy of the expedition archives.

Interior photo spread: All photos courtesy of the expedition archives. Current photos of expedition members: Simon Jackson (Monica Jackson), Coppinger and Associates (Elizabeth Stark) and Myrtle Simpson (Evelyn Camrass). Photo of Arlene Blum: John Percival.

Library of Congress Cataloging-in-Publication Data
Jackson, Monica.
  Tents in the clouds : the first women's Himalayan expedition by Monica Jackson and Elizabeth Stark.—U.S. ed.
      p. cm.
  Originally published: England : Collins, 1956.
  ISBN 1-58005-033-6 (pbk.)
    1. Women mountaineers—Himalaya Mountains. 2. Mountaineering—Himalaya Mountains. 3. Himalaya Mountains—Description and travel.
  I. Stark, Elizabeth. II. Title.
  GV199.44.H55 J33 2000   796.52'2'092—dc21   99-053880

Printed in Canada

First printing, January 2000

10 9 8 7 6 5 4 3 2 1

Distributed to the trade by Publishers Group West
In Canada: Publishers Group West Canada, Toronto, Ontario
In the U.K. and Europe: Airlift Book Company, Middlesex, England
In Australia: Banyan Tree Book Distributors, Kent Town, South Australia

Dedicated to
ESMÉ
who did not come

Acknowledgments

We should like to acknowledge our debt to the following: The members of the Mount Everest Foundation for their moral support. Those members of the Scottish Mountaineering Club who gave us encouragement and a great deal of practical advice. The firms who generously supplied us with their goods free or on special terms.

We thank them all heartily.

Contents

Contents

Maps

Chief Dates

1955

April 10th	Arrived Kathmandu
April 13th	Journey started
April 19th	Arrived Tempathang
April 22nd	Arrived Base Camp
April 24th	Departed on first exploration of Phurbi Chyachumbu glacier
April 29th	Returned to Base Camp
May 2nd	Found pass leading to Dorje Lakpa glacier
May 5th	Departed on second exploratory trip up glacier
May 8th	Reached first col on Frontier Ridge
May 9th	Started up Ladies' Glacier
May 11th	Climbed Gyalgen Peak
May 14th	Arrived back at Base Camp
May 17th	Betty and Monica departed for Dorje Lakpa glacier and Western Jugal Himal. Evelyn departed for Chaksil Danda Ridge
May 21st	Party reunited at Pemsal
May 25th	Reached Panch Pokhari
June 1st	Returned to Kathmandu

FOREWORD

by Arlene Blum

IN THE spring of 1955, a team of three British women mountaineers climbed in the Jugal Himal, a range of wild and unexplored peaks perched on the border between Nepal and Tibet. With slim resources but enormous joy and spirit they found a way to these remote peaks and made the first ascent of a twenty-two-thousand-foot peak, which they named Gyalgen after Mingma Gyalgen, their lead Sherpa. Monica Jackson, Elizabeth Stark and Dr. Evelyn Camrass went down in history as the first team of women ever to climb in the Himalaya.

Their story remains current and compelling today, nearly half a century after the book was originally published in Britain in 1956. The vivid quality of the writing allows us to share with the team their delight at meeting the gracious people of Nepal, the uncertainty of finding their way into this previously untrodden territory and their pleasure at sharing hard work and lighthearted antics with the Sherpas who assisted them. According to the authors, best of all were " the days of strenuous endeavor we spent on the high ridges, glaciers and snowfields of the Jugal that will remain for ever in our memories as not only the happiest, but also, strangely enough, the most serene and peaceful days of our lives. "

Foreword

To fully appreciate what these three climbers achieved, it is worth setting their expedition in the context of the exploration of the Himalaya at the time. Nepal first opened its doors to the outside world in 1950. That year a valiant French team made the historic ascent of Annapurna I, the first summit ever reached over the magical height of 8000 meters. This team, led by Maurice Herzog, had an incorrect map and spent weeks struggling just to find Annapurna. The monsoon season was fast approaching when they finally located the mountain. Miraculously, they managed to reach the summit and get everyone back down alive in spite of avalanches, exhaustion and a raging storm. Their success is one of the most dramatic stories in the history of mountaineering.

It was only five years later that Jackson, Stark and Dr. Camrass mounted their expedition into the precipitous Jugal Himal. Their maps were similarly inaccurate and the access into the Jugal uncertain. Compared with today's high-tech gear, their clothing and equipment were heavy and awkward. Nonetheless with high spirits they overcame all obstacles and hardships to achieve their goal.

Their account will inspire anyone who reads it— putting together a pioneering expedition, crossing unknown country to find their mountains, vivid encounters with storms, forest fire, drunken Sherpas, the problems of finding privacy on the glacier, tracking the Yeti, all are described with humor and honesty.

Jackson and Stark also explore the " strange compulsion . . . that induced two sensible women to give up their jobs, and a third to part from a beloved family, to subject themselves to extremes of discomfort and possibly to risk their lives, creeping up and down some singularly lonely, alien and desolate wrinkles on the earth's surface. "

I so wish I had known about this book in the 1960s when I myself began to dream of going on expeditions to distant realms. But the pioneering efforts of this and several other hardy groups of British women climbers in the 1950s were unknown in the American climbing community.

In 1969, I applied to go on a guided expedition to Denali and was told that women could only go as far as the base camp to help with the cooking. When I questioned this, the leader informed me that women lacked the necessary physical strength and emotional stability to climb high peaks. I wish I could have told him about the daring mountain exploits recounted in *Tents in the Clouds*.

In 1970, I helped organize an all-women team of climbers who did succeed in climbing Denali. In addition to the challenges of reaching the arctic summit of the highest mountain in North America, we faced the prejudices of the time about women's limitations. This book would have encouraged us and made it easier for us to accomplish our climb, just as it should today inspire anyone undertaking a challenging adventure.

When I read *Tents in the Clouds* it brought back memories of the Denali trip and also our 1978 women's expedition to Annapurna—the challenge of attempting something that women weren't supposed to be able to do, the extraordinary beauty of the high mountains and the satisfaction of working together as a team to reach a goal more challenging than we had believed we could possibly achieve.

Foreword

Their story exemplifies what a small team of individuals can accomplish with vision, passion and determination. My thanks to Monica Jackson, Elizabeth Stark and Dr. Evelyn Camrass for sharing their remarkable adventure and to Seal Press for making this unforgettable story available to a new generation.

Arlene Blum
Berkeley, California
September 1999

PROLOGUE

by Monica Jackson

IN THE spring of 1955, three of us, obscure mountaineers
with no claim to fame, became the first expedition composed entirely of women ever to explore and climb in the
high Himalaya. This is how it happened:

To begin with, I should like to make it clear that the
" first ever " aspect was quite unpremeditated. It was not
until our plans had already begun to take shape that it
occurred to us that we were creating a precedent. Plenty
of women, including myself, had already climbed in the
Himalaya, and the significance of the fact that we had all
done so as members of expeditions led by men at first
escaped us entirely. Of course, when we realised that we
would be pioneering in more senses than one, we were
quite pleased, since it seemed to us that this might improve our chances of obtaining financial backing. On the
other hand, we thought it would mean that we would
have to contend with a good deal of prejudice at first.
Both these surmises proved correct.

As it turned out, we succeeded in doing all we had
hoped to do—which was to find a way through the lower
gorges to the glacier valleys of the Jugal Himal, to find a
way up the glaciers into the heart of the group, to find
passes over the mountain ridges separating one glacier
from another, to check and correct the accuracy of the map
we had—for we were going into untrodden territory,

only surveyed from afar—in fact to explore the last large unexplored area of the Nepal Himalaya. We also climbed an unmapped mountain and gave it a name.

In 1954 I was asked to give a talk to the Ladies' Scottish Climbing Club, of which I was a new member. My theme was that, contrary to general belief, there was nothing particularly esoteric about Himalayan climbing for experienced mountaineers of either sex, and that Sherpas, provided they were treated with respect and good manners, would not give women climbers any more trouble than they were liable to give men. After the lecture Betty Stark and Evelyn Camrass cornered me, and we spent the rest of the evening eagerly discussing a hypothetical all-women expedition, which was to include a fourth member of the club, Esmé Speakman, a seasoned Alpinist.

Thereafter the project seemed to grow almost of its own volition. It was discussed by Betty and Evelyn in a tent in Arctic Norway and by Esmé and me in mountain huts in Switzerland. Later, sentences beginning, " I've just thought of something else we ought to do . . . " were shouted from stance to stance on rock climbs in Glencoe and on Ben Nevis, and blown away by the gale on misty Highland ridges. Plans were argued out over sodden sandwiches as we crouched shivering behind boulders in snowstorms on Scottish mountains. And agreements were reached by candlelight over cups of tea in Scottish climbing-huts. Within a year, despite doubts and set-backs, our adventure had taken shape and was gaining momentum. Like a magic carpet woven by our own labour, it would carry us at last to the roof of the world, those " ultimate mountains, " the Himalaya.

And then, at the last moment, illness prevented Esmé from coming. It was a cruel disappointment for her and a great blow to the rest of us. She was our most experienced climber, our best photographer, and the only one of us who knew anything about surveying. Some indication of the respect we all had for her is shown by the fact that though she did not accompany us, we always thought of her as part of the expedition.

The three of us who remained were people of widely differing backgrounds and personalities. But we had this in common—a love of mountains and of the wild places of the earth, and a knowledge of and respect for the art of mountaineering. Evelyn, a recently qualified doctor, Betty, then a speech therapist and teacher, and I, then a freelance journalist, wife and mother, appreciative though we were of our good fortune throughout the period of our venture, had no idea of how privileged we were to travel in those mountains in those pristine days. Competition and commercialisation have smeared a trail of human detritus across the face of some of the earth's most beautiful places. Since they are no longer inaccessible, the sheer weight of human traffic has tended to sour relations between the hill-people and their visitors. Exploration is confined to harder and harder routes on individual mountains. Of course, the peaks are still there to take the breath away from new generations of aspirants, but how blessed the three of us were to go when we did, to tread untrodden snows and to change the map.

All that was over forty years ago. Where, and who, are we now? Betty, who lives in the United States with her husband, has retired from a professorial chair. Evelyn and I still live in our native Scotland. She, retired from her gynaecological consultancy, with children and grandchildren to keep her busy, still climbs and skis. I have also been blessed with grandchildren, and, retired with a doctorate in anthropology, have switched my researches from social and demographic studies to seeking the interface between science and metaphysics. In a way we are still exploring.

I have often been asked that question familiar to all female mountaineers to this day: what strange compulsion was it that induced two sensible women to give up their jobs, and a third to part from a beloved family, to subject themselves to extremes of discomfort and possibly to risk their lives, creeping up and down some singularly lonely, alien and desolate wrinkles on the earth's surface? If there is a precise answer I do not know it. We certainly did not go in search of excitement, though excitement sometimes came our way, nor to pit ourselves deliberately against more formidable hazards than we had hitherto faced. I think that we, in common with most mountaineers who go to climb in the Himalaya, went there on a sort of pilgrimage.

As far as I am concerned these lines by Matthew Arnold provide an apology, if not an explanation.

Ye are bound for the mountains?
Ah! With you let me go,
Where yon cold distant barrier
The vast range of snow
Through its loose clouds lifts dimly
Its white peaks in air:
How deep is the stillness:
Ah! would I were there.

PART ONE

by Elizabeth Stark

CHAPTER ONE

Cloak and Dagger

O UR EXPEDITION was barely two months in the field,
but it took us nine months to plan it. We could not
pretend to be brilliant climbers but we could organise
thoroughly and carefully. None of us was a model of
efficiency, and this detailed work, which had to be fitted in
with our professions or the care of a house and family, often
went against the grain ; but if we slipped up and so got into
trouble, there were plenty of people who would say, "These
women should never have been allowed out in the mountains
on their own." We did not mean to give them the chance.

We had no leader, in fact it never occurred to us to have
one, and since we are all individual in character we probably
co-operated better so than if one of us *had* been in command.
We were all of the same mind in most things to do with the
expedition and when decisions had to be taken in the field
there was always a casting vote.

Our first major problem was the choice of area. Some
of the most delightful parts of the Himalaya, in Garhwal and
Sikkim for instance, had been put out of bounds to us by the
Indian Government's " Inner Line." The Karakoram
offered many real giants but, though tempting, was likely to
be expensive and too difficult for us. That left Kulu and
Nepal. There were unexplored areas and unclimbed peaks
in Kulu, and we were told that many of those nearing the
20,000 foot mark were less formidable than peaks of this

height in other ranges. But the approaches to this area seemed too "popular." In the Nepal Himalaya, on the other hand, we should encounter terrific gorges, little-known country and peaks so strongly fortified throughout thousands of feet that the question of climbing them would not arise. In the end we decided to go to Nepal. It would be a bigger adventure, possibly even too big.

But the whole northern frontier of Nepal, 500 miles long, is on the main Himalayan chain, therefore we had to narrow the choice down much further. To this end we consulted Douglas Scott, an experienced member of two Scottish Himalayan expeditions, who has a flair for hatching exciting, exacting mountain plans. His finger went unerringly to a great loop in the Himalayan chain north-east of Kathmandu.

" You know, nothing much has been done there," he said reflectively, " I've had my eye on that part of the world for a long time myself."

Further research showed that this loop comprised the Langtang Himal, which Tilman visited in 1949 on one of the first mountaineering expeditions ever allowed into Nepal, and the Jugal Himal. Tilman's party had explored the Langtang Himal pretty thoroughly but had climbed none of the peaks there. They were hampered by poor snow conditions and cloud during the monsoon. The area had not been visited since and no one at all had been to the Jugal Himal, a horse-shoe-shaped range of mountains, which, as far as we could discover, was the last great unexplored area left in Nepal.

This state of affairs seemed strange to us since the Langtang Himal and the Jugal Himal lie nearer to Kathmandu than any other part of the Nepal Himalaya. But there were two good reasons for the neglect of these areas. When Nepal was first opened to mountaineers, expeditions naturally tended to gravitate towards the giants of its great ranges, particularly in the Everest region, whereas the highest peak in the Langtang-Jugal area is well under 24,000 feet in height. Secondly, though lower in height, these peaks were not easy, the only reports of them being far from encouraging.

We were intrigued to learn that Tilman had found a pass from the Langtang Himal through to the Jugal Himal, without being able to penetrate this second range. He followed a glacier on the far side of the pass and camped on its lower reaches.

Tents in the Clouds

" Early in the morning," he writes, " before the clouds rolled up, Tensing and I climbed on to the moraine to see where we were. Not far away the glacier terminated and its waters drained south-east into a deep gorge. Beyond we could make out the dark cleft of the main valley, to all appearances an even deeper gorge, where, the rivers still running high, we could count upon meeting all sorts of trouble. . . . If (this) main valley could not be reached from above, why should we not enter it from below, from the nearest village? According to the map there was a village called Tempathang on the east side of the valley close to a bridge, whence, from our experience of the Langtang and the Ganesh, we might expect to find a track to some high alp in the heart of the Jugal Himal."

He followed this course, but unsuccessfully. On contacting the natives of Tempathang, he found that " They could give us nothing but green mealie cobs and, what was worse, the information that there was no path up the valley; for their grazing alps had long since been abandoned, the track to them through long disuse and fallen bridges being no longer passable."

We decided to go direct to Tempathang and first of all to find out more about the approaches, if any, to the Jugal Himal. We hoped for little from this line of inquiry, for Tilman adds . . . " From a latter glimpse we had of them, they (the Jugal peaks) seemed as uncompromising as the Langtang peaks and far less approachable."

The second and major part of our plan was concerned with crossing by Tilman's pass over to the Langtang. We hoped to visit the cols he had discovered there overlooking Tibet, in clear weather, taking bearings and augmenting the photographic record of the area.

To carry out this plan successfully we must avoid the monsoon, with its heavy cloud and swollen rivers, and either go before it in the spring or after it in the autumn. Spring used to be the season most generally favoured for climbing in the Himalaya, but though cloud contrasts and Alpine flowers make it a lovely time of the year it is also a time of storm and avalanche. Apart from one or two big storms, autumn weather is more settled, the mountains assuming a static theatrical appearance, like huge cumbersome pieces of stage furniture. Great cold and darkness however drive the climber into his sleeping-bag earlier each day. After weighing these considerations carefully, and a further one, that we had better go soon or we should not go at all, we settled for the spring.

The first decisive step was taken when we placed our project before the Screening Committee of the Joint Himalayan Committee of the Royal Geographical Society and the Alpine Club (now replaced by the Mount Everest Foundation). It was only through the good offices of this august body that we could hope to gain a permit to enter Nepal, especially as, in view of recent unrest in the country, the Nepalese authorities might be unwilling to countenance an all-woman party.

We were not very hopeful about our chances of obtaining the Himalayan Committee's recommendation, because of our sex, and because we were nowhere near the top flight of British climbers. To our amazement and gratitude, we found neither of these considerations seemed to weigh with them as much as what we and our referees were able to tell them about our general experience of mountaineering and mountain travel.

We were recommended through the Foreign Office to the British Embassy in Kathmandu, who were in direct contact with the Foreign Affairs Department in Nepal.

Understandably enough, other people in authority did not show the same reassuring faith in our ability to bring

off such a venture unscathed. Some thought that we would
never reach the mountains at all but be murdered, robbed
or raped by brigands on the way. Those who were better
informed knew that we could travel with perfect safety
among the friendly people of the foothills, but thought we
should certainly come to grief among the mountains themselves. Others again thought that the Sherpas, whose
outlook has altered radically since the conquest of Everest
has brought them into the limelight, would desert us at
some crucial point on the march.

Months elapsed before we heard that our application
would not be put forward to the Nepalese unless we were
given a *further very strong recommendation*. Our mountaineering
experience was all very well, but what, it was asked, would
we do with a drunken Sherpa?

Monica replied with conviction that Esmé Speakman had
been with a welfare unit during the war, which followed
the liberation army into Holland and Germany. That
when Evelyn and I were climbing in Arctic Norway we
found that the chief hazard there was the persistent atten-
tions of drunken Sea-Lapps in our valley camps and that
we had emerged from our predicament with honour and
international relations unimpaired. She herself had spent
a great deal of her life in India, and spoke Hindustani
fluently if ungrammatically. She had got on well with the
Sherpas on her previous Himalayan expedition, acting as
liaison between the leader and the sirdar.

A further fact emerged quite fortuitously, helping to turn
the scales in our favour. I had hitch-hiked to the Alps one
year with another girl, coping *en route* with Communist
lorry-drivers, an emotional attorney and a travelling
circus.

This time our application went forward to the Nepalese
authorities. It was likely we would hear no more about it

until we were ready to sail, so we had to get ahead with the detailed work of organisation.

We had neglected one important maxim laid down by W. H. Murray in the following words, " You must . . . face the brutal fact that if you want to go, say, to the Himalaya, you must first of all save up at least three hundred and fifty pounds, or else persuade someone to give it to you. Until that is done you cannot move."

That was in 1951. Now costs have risen in the Himalaya and you may need four hundred and fifty pounds (each).

We had not actually moved without any money at all. Esmé Speakman, though compelled to withdraw herself, had made us a generous loan but we still did not have anything like enough to run an expedition. Nor did we have the time to save it up, so we resorted to persuading someone to give it to us.

This was Monica's job since she lived in London, and it was a ticklish one. Though we knew we could arouse a certain amount of interest by the very fact that we were the first all-woman expedition to the Himalaya, we did not want to become a cheap stunt. We owe it to a certain sporting instinct in editorial and publishing worlds that we ever got into the Jugal Himal at all. But it was not until very near the day of departure that this problem was finally solved.

Monica also arranged for the four Sherpas we required, not as guides . . . no one can act as guide to an unexplored area in any case . . . but to carry loads to high camps. She insured them, applied for duty free entry permits, export licences, Bank of England permission to take enough money into Nepal, and maps. She began to see everything in triplicate, relieved occasionally by quadruplicate.

My job was to plan food supplies, order all the expedition equipment and draw up lists of personal equipment for each one of us.

Tents in the Clouds

Stuart Bain of Messrs. Andrew Lusk and Co., Ltd., who had much experience in packing for expeditions to Everest, Kanchenjunga and the Antarctic, undertook to pack and ship our stores and some of the equipment. At his suggestion I drew up a packing plan, dividing the food so that the assortment in each crate was enough for one week. Then if one crate fell into a raging torrent, we should not at one stroke lose all our soup or jam. Quite a different assortment had to be made up for those weeks when we should be in the mountains, featuring more high-altitude rations.

This job was more difficult than one would imagine for, just as I had achieved a really beautiful set of permutations, Stuart Bain would point out, " You can't have a pound of biscuits in crate No. 7. Biscuits only come in 2 lb. tins." Or Evelyn, who began like Tigger by saying she liked everything, would look over my shoulder and qualify this statement as far as nearly every item on my list was concerned. " We should have treats," she would conclude, " in case we ever feel low." And judging by the number and variety of treats suggested, she did not expect to be particularly cheerful. Then Monica would comment plaintively, " You've only got twenty-four tins of sardines. I *like* sardines."

Our climbing equipment had to be modest, including only such items as were absolutely essential. We could not afford eiderdown suits and fortunately oxygen was not necessary at the heights we should reach.

One heavy expense was the Sherpas' equipment, which we would have to give to them. We did not know that Sherpas are much more demanding nowadays, and took only second-hand stuff for ours.

In the past, Scottish expeditions triumphantly raided the Glasgow Barrows, a market like Petticoat Lane, where boots, wind-proof suits, kit-bags and goggles could all be unearthed for a mere song. But those halcyon days are gone. All I could discover were a few woollen semmits. I dare say our Sherpas were the first ever to receive these articles washed, aired and mended by the expedition members themselves.

I had a stroke of luck, however, in hearing of some men's long underpants going at a sale, and a fellow member of the Ladies' Scottish Climbing Club dashed off and joined the queue four successive times (they were sold singly) to secure these prizes.

Many firms supplied us with food and equipment, free or on special terms. Several manufacturers actually pointed out that we had not asked them for enough and this was especially generous, for Himalayan expeditions were beginning to be two a penny and all seemed to be in the same state of beggary as ourselves.

Indeed, apart from the initial difficulties of having our project accepted, everyone, business people, civil servants, British, Indian and Nepalese officials, was most helpful, and many arrangements and permits were specially expedited for us. There is no doubt that our sex was a positive advantage, although we never tried to use it as such nor to get special treatment. People were genuinely interested in our venture, or at the very least did not want to be responsible for getting us into difficulties, or to have us on their hands if we did.

Evelyn, who had the least time of any of us to spare from her duties in a maternity hospital, studied tropical medicine, arranged for us to be variously injected and, with the invaluable help of doctors and pharmacists who had been to the Himalaya, ordered and packed our drugs and medical equipment. I felt it was grossly unfair that I could not criticise her lists in my turn, since they dealt with mysteries beyond my ken. But when Evelyn said loftily, " I have enough antacid under my bed to sink a battleship," I was able to reply sharply, " I have enough dried vegetables under mine to feed the expedition, which is more to the point."

Finally, I had to list and value everything over and over again for the United Kingdom High Commission in New Delhi, for packers, Indian Customs, Board of Trade, the P. & O. Steamship Navigation Company, and, it seemed, their friends. We were tempted to exercise new-found cunning and value each item twice over, once for the Customs in case we lost it and had to pay the stated value, and once for the Insurance people in case we lost it and had to be paid. At the last moment it was discovered we had no pot-scrubbers and no soap.

It was difficult in the thick of all this to keep in good training and this was especially important in view of the shortness of the march from Kathmandu to our chosen area. Evelyn and I went climbing or ski-ing at week-ends as often as we could and left it at that. Monica, living in London, was unable to get away to the hills so often, but in despair over this made greater efforts than either Evelyn or myself. She rose on winter mornings to run round Regent's Park when it was still so dark she was tripping over the ducks—a procedure amply justified by results. It occurs to me, too, that it is not laughable to write " Housewife " as occupation when applying for permission to climb in the Himalaya. It is the sedentary job which keeps one in poor training.

We tried to observe great secrecy over our plans. This was because we feared undue publicity or mis-representation in the Press, since our plans were modest and might in any case come to nothing. We called ourselves at this time the " Cloak and Dagger Expedition " and Evelyn, to whom secretiveness is quite foreign, enjoyed this immensely, giving out dark hints and telling most of our friends in the strictest confidence all about it.

Cloak and Dagger

The news leaked out from Kathmandu when our permit was finally granted. We had to adjust ourselves to the idea that we were now actually going, and to a further disturbing fact. When the official announcement reached us, we discovered that our permit was for the Jugal Himal only. Raymond Lambert, with a Belgian scientist, had been given permission to visit the Langtang Himal and the Nepal Government, quite rightly, do not care to have more than one expedition in a particular valley at any one time for fear of disturbing local economy.

This meant a drastic last-minute change of plan. We would *have* to find a way into the Jugal Himal.

We had arranged to pick up the relevant maps of Nepal in New Delhi for the expedition, but the Indian Government will not allow these out of their country, and so far as we knew none of our area was available in the United Kingdom. Monica had now joined the Royal Geographical Society, and discovered that all the maps of Nepal could be referred to in its library.

The map of the Jugal Himal seemed to confirm Tilman's report of it. There were no villages near the mountains proper—Tempathang is at 8,000 feet—and no passes over the main range. In this, the area was unlike the Langtang Himal or the Everest region. The answer seemed to be that the Balephi Khola, the river running from the heart of the Jugal, and its tributaries, were colossal gorges. We would probably have to spend days fighting our way up each side stream until we could cross it, then down again on the other side, having porter trouble all the way.

The inside of the Jugal horse-shoe seemed to be another Nanda Devi sanctuary, and Heaven knew whether we would ever be able to penetrate it or to get out whole again if we did.

CHAPTER TWO

A Changing Kathmandu

WE ARRIVED in Bombay on Saturday, the second of April, and were met on board ship by an elderly Parsee in a shiny black hat. He introduced himself to us as the agent whom we had engaged to help us through the Customs formalities, and our hearts sank, for he was not at all the high-powered, smooth, efficient sort of fellow we had expected. We soon found that high-powered efficiency is as nothing compared with patience and deviousness when it comes to getting through the Indian Customs, and came to look on this gentleman as an old friend.

But first we had to get hold of some baggage to go through the Customs with. The P. & O. Steamship Navigation Company must have become used to thinking of expeditions in terms of the tons of crates and bales which Everest or Kanchenjunga demand, for they have made a ruling that all expeditions must send their gear as cargo. Our few bits and pieces must have looked very insignificant in the hold.

But cargo, we were now told, was always taken ashore on small barges which might hang about the harbour for days, to be discharged finally on some far-distant wharf. A fat, cross little man said they might be on a barge already. Future expeditions as small as ours might be well advised to put down their gear as household effects—as by a stretch of imagination they are, for if one is so eccentric as to set

34

up house on a glacier, Primuses, arctic sleeping-bags and ropes become important items of furniture.

On Monday we found our thirty-two boxes safely stacked on the pier, but they were now in the hands of the Customs who were in no hurry to part with them. A complicated bond had to be executed if we were not to pay 100 per cent duty on everything we had. Haunted by the thought of an early monsoon and a retreat from the mountains cut off by fierce, swollen torrents, we did not make the mistake of relying on charm but produced lists and permits faster than they could be demanded. These were the right tactics, for the officials expected us to be pretty clueless and our preparedness fairly bowled them over. By the end of the day they had exhausted the drama of the situation and the boxes were ours. It was something of a record.

In the hour or so left to us we changed, packed personal stuff and triumphantly caught the Frontier Mail for Delhi. The friends we had been staying with saw us go with undisguised relief. We offered to send them photographs. "We've had quite enough of this expedition, thank you," they answered faintly. In the days following, we began to feel very much the same.

As we progressed northwards across a plain like a vast, cracked slab of concrete the stations became smaller and pokier, the time allowed for us to fetch out our thirty-two boxes at each change of train, shorter.

In the ladies' waiting-room at Lucknow were sundry gentlemen, for whom the women in purdah perfunctorily lowered their veils. There was a gentlemen's waiting-room as well, occupied by chatting ladies, so it did not seem to matter a great deal which one chose. Monkeys screeched at the windows, and the main station was smelly, noisy and unbearably hot. It is a comment on the subsequent lowering of our standards that, when we returned to Lucknow two months or so later, Evelyn cried, " Oh! What a lovely station! "

We reached our lowest ebb at Saguali Junction, an outpost not far from the frontier of Nepal, lying in the hot, malarial plain of the Terai. We arrived an hour late for our connection. The station-master would have held this connection up if he had had any influence with it, but Indian trains are more rigid about their time-tables now than they used to be. We spent most of the day in the " Upper Class Ladies' Waiting Room," lying on our tarpaulin. Evelyn and I had been quite unable to understand the mentality of the people who lay about in swarms on streets and platforms in India. Now we were reduced to very much the same condition ourselves, and found it too much of an effort even to swat the innumerable flies.

The evening train came at last and took us across the hazy, moonlit Terai to Raxaul on the frontier of India and Nepal. A young member of the aristocratic Rana family of Nepal, returning on leave from the Indian Merchant Navy, had become attached to us by this time, calling us " Sister " and bringing us souvenirs and photographs—one of the interior of a Rana palace, showing a huge portrait of Queen Victoria hanging above various royal personages of Nepal. He talked without ceasing about religion and his country's politics, and sang us songs from Japan, Yugoslavia and the Broomielaw. We were too exhausted to pay any attention.

In Raxaul a genial little Nepali with a stutter conducted us to the Indian Embassy bungalow, where we washed in a big, noisy, tin bath and fell asleep at once under tattered mosquito nets.

We had decided to fly across the jungles of the Terai and the foothills to Kathmandu. There was no motor road to the capital at that time, though the Indian Army was building one wide enough to take three-ton lorries, which was completed just in time to be partly washed away by the monsoon rains. The only alternative to flying was to walk over the bridle paths, which rise to about 7,000 feet then drop to the valley of Kathmandu, and which for centuries were the only link between it and the outside world. We wanted to make this traditional approach but it takes two days, or more if the rope-way which takes the luggage should be over-worked or on holiday—and it seemed to be both on our arrival.

Nepalis are so jealous of their land that they will not always allow permanent structures to be built on it by foreign concerns and regard even mission hospitals with suspicion. There were only grass huts at the air-strip, no control tower and no radio. One pilot took another, a Sikh new to the route, aside. He pointed vaguely to the mist and we were horrified to hear him say, "You make for that valley and then follow it."

We twisted in and out among the hills, turning almost as sharply sometimes as at a street corner. Even when we emerged from these valleys we could not see the mountains beyond, for they were wrapped in cloud, but we were content to wait for them.

When we touched down in Kathmandu, we felt we had reached a promised land. In the best tradition of younger sons with their fortunes to seek, we had carried out the well-nigh impossible tasks, obeyed the mysterious injunctions and earned a great reward.

The fertile valley of Kathmandu lies at about 4,500 feet and is nine miles wide and fifteen miles long. The three and a half per cent of the population which can read and write is concentrated there and, politically speaking, it is the only part of Nepal which counts, the rest of the country being too remote and too backward to hold opinions or to care who is in power.

Tents in the Clouds

For centuries this valley was land-locked in the Himalaya and sealed off from the rest of the world by a ban on foreigners, which the ruling family, the Ranas, had imposed. They hoped to prevent their country from becoming contaminated with Western ways of life, and no one can blame them entirely for that, but this was partly because Western ideas would have threatened their absolute authority. The valley was never cut off from India, however, and gradually through Radio Delhi, Indian newspapers and the few travellers who did succeed in getting permission to enter Nepal, notions spread about land reforms and elections, and finally, in 1950–51, the oppressive rule of the Ranas was broken. The King, who had been a mere puppet, kept because, as the incarnation of the God Vishnu, he was indispensable to religious ceremonies, became the true head of the state.

This King died just before we left for India, and many citizens were still going about with their heads shaved in mourning when we arrived in Kathmandu. His son, who was spoken of as a capable and earnest man, has succeeded him, but he is faced with a difficult task. He is trying to by-pass centuries of evolution and make a modern state of Nepal in the face of 150,000 politically-minded citizens who have formed themselves into no less than sixty-nine splinter groups, and an administration of public services so inefficient it can hardly be said to exist.

Our only experience of this administration was on the day before we left, when we were trying to get a Nepalese driving licence for Evelyn as a souvenir. The crux of the test is a question on the Highway Code, " What would you do if you saw the royal car approaching? "

" Slow down and stop," replied Evelyn at random.

" Excellent. You have passed with flying flags. You may have your licence in a few weeks' time."

At the police station, where we tried to expedite matters,

38

there were milling crowds and anyone who had secured a job was sitting with his feet up contemplating his good fortune. Evelyn's signature was regarded as a dubious characteristic, and a thumb-print and evidence of birthmarks were demanded as well.

We were met at the airport by Mr. Price of the British Embassy, and the manager of the hotel where we were to stay. With them was our Sherpa sirdar, Mingma Gyalgen, proudly sweating in his boots and balaclava, the marks of his trade. We liked him at once, and he seemed delighted to see us and gave us a warm handshake. He had just returned from carrying a load to Kanchenjunga, and brought good wishes from Tom McKinnon of the Kanchenjunga team. " I know Mingma well," he wrote, " you couldn't have a better man."

We were introduced to the Commander-in-Chief of the Nepalese Army and the Minister of Foreign Affairs. Neither wore those resplendent uniforms of the nineteenth century we had read about, which combined features of the English dragoon's and the French hussar's all mixed up with oriental finery, glittering slippers and jewelled sabres. Yet both were men of erect military bearing and so polished in their address that we felt extremely uncomfortable in our travelling jeans.

We were wafted through the Nepalese Customs and bundled into a lorry with all our gear. One or two smiling Nepalis jumped in as well, trying to look as if they had been specially appointed to mind the gear, though it turned out they were cadging a lift.

It was from the top of this lorry, bumping and swaying and embracing one another involuntarily, that we formed our first impression of Kathmandu. We saw the huge, colonnaded palaces which had belonged to the Ranas when in power, some of them offices now, neglected-looking and needing a coat of paint; and the temples congregating in open squares, rich in design, for the Newari craftsmen who built them were inspired by Hinduism and Buddhism, by the art of India and the art of China; and the dwelling-houses which have finely carved walls and window-frames, and strange idols as corner-stones. These houses, built by men of a small race, have cramped staircases and match-box rooms on each story, and indoors even the Nepalis have to mind their heads. The whole city was much more spread out and grubby than photographs had led us to expect, but we liked it none the less.

The citizens wore cotton jodhpur-like trousers, a shirt hanging over them with side pockets below the waist, and the little Nepali hats of black material or stiffened gay-coloured cotton. But these hats are for men only and we caused a good deal of amusement when we tried them on in the bazaar. The women wear saris, and some of the upper class women we saw were heavily powdered to look pale, and heavily rouged.

The hotel was rough and ready—just the place, in fact, for the headquarters of a Himalayan expedition. There was no such accommodation, and no need for it, in Kathmandu until two or three years ago. Even in 1949 very few foreigners were being allowed into the country. But now it has become comparatively easy for tourists to get a visa for Nepal and soon they will be attracted to Kathmandu and the surrounding places of interest in increasing numbers. Already there is talk of a youth hostel in the city, of picture postcards and of another hotel near the air-strip at Pokhra, of which Longstaff wrote in 1949, " Mysterious Pokhra, tropical, low-lying, and closely backed by the immense peaks of Annapurna, is still beyond our ken."

We had much to do and ran about in the hotel manager's

40

jeep, though petrol is almost as expensive as whisky in Kathmandu.

First we went to see the Deputy-Secretary who was to appoint a liaison officer to our party. The Nepal Government now insists on all expeditions taking a liaison officer with them, to act as interpreter and help in dealings with the local people. We had imagined that this man would be a sturdy Gurkha N.C.O., bristling with kukris and other weapons. Now we were told that he was to be a young student who would soon be able to speak English well, and who would like to have some instruction in natural history and mountaineering. To the natural history we assented feebly, but we felt we could not promise to take a beginner with us on what might turn out to be difficult and dangerous glaciers. Besides we had no mountaineering equipment for the lad. Finally it was agreed that he should go to base-camp only.

We came to the conclusion that the Nepal Government, besides wishing to help expeditions, were anxious for their intelligent young citizens to widen their experience and incidentally bring back news of the people in remoter villages who have little contact with officialdom. This was very praiseworthy but we could not help feeling a little disgruntled that it was to cost *us* two hundred Indian rupees (nearly £30) a month.

We now had to visit the bank, cash travellers' cheques and amass a great deal of coin, for it was possible that paper money would not be acceptable in the farther villages along our route. A clerk spread about a hundred pounds' worth on the floor for us, the coins spinning from his hand into rows of bright rosettes, while the bank manager discoursed on foreign stamps. These seem to interest many Nepalis, perhaps because Nepal is not a member of the World Postal Union, having only an internal postal service of its own.

This must give them a great advantage when it comes to swaps.

Meanwhile Evelyn, with our Sherpas, was sorting all our equipment into loads. They lashed tents, ropes, and so on, to our boxes, making up loads which the porters seemed to find as comfortable as sixty pounds plus their own gear could be expected to feel. We had brought with us a shining new spring-balance but we were so impressed with the accuracy of Mingma's hand and eye in estimating loads that we left this gadget behind, and had no reason later to regret it.

All this gave Evelyn a splendid opportunity to become acquainted with our Sherpas and, when Monica and I arrived on the scene, we found her getting along very well with them, though she could not speak to any of them, except Mingma, who had a little English.

Mingma was quiet and well-mannered and showed a lot of common sense, though we wondered at first if he would have sufficient authority with his men. His Himalayan Club book showed that he had had a lot of experience both as a climbing Sherpa and as a sirdar, on Everest, Cho Oyu, Gauri-Sankar and many other mountains. It also said that he was an excellent cook, and having sampled my cuisine, and being unwilling to undertake the kitchen chores themselves, Monica and Evelyn read this with undisguised satisfaction.

With him Mingma had brought his cousin, Ang Temba. Ang Temba was a high-spirited young man, and just could not suppress his natural bonhomie. He was the least experienced of our Sherpas and we thought he might prove impetuous, needing a firm hand on the mountain. In this we were right.

Chhepela was the only one who still wore his hair in a Tibetan-style pigtail, plaited into red wool and wound round his head. We liked this about him, and also his reserve. We heard later that he had been considered a moody fellow on Everest, but we did not see this side of him. Quite soon he proved intelligent. We never had to tell him anything twice and if he was interested in any item of equipment, a special torch or a compass, he would take it away and learn how to work it for himself.

Not so poor Kusung. He had been with several expeditions in the past, but the last one recorded in his book was that led by Shipton in 1936. We wondered why there were no subsequent entries. He was, however, very willing, so willing he would come dashing up, eager to see what he could do for us, then turn away with disappointment written all over his honest face, having failed to notice, say, three dirty mugs lying on the table. Whenever we saw Kusung coming to help, we said, " Oh, Lord," and pretended to be doing nothing after all. But we became very fond of him. Dear old Kusung! He was so wonderfully comic, except perhaps when he was trying to be comic.

With our Sherpas were Kusung's nephew, Bahu, and his little daughter, Ang Droma. Bahu was a square young man who was always making anxious-sounding little noises to himself, even when he was perfectly happy. But Ang Droma was the bright one of the family. She was a sweet little person, about sixteen years old, and the first time we met her she came confidingly up to us, put her ear to my watch and laughed with delight. She carried a load almost as big as herself without complaining and, since she was the only other woman in the party, she had a special place in our affection. These two were to come with us as porters.

None of the Sherpas seemed to mind taking instructions from women in the least. In fact they were rather tickled with the idea. They knew that they had been specially chosen to come with us as reliable men, and this was enough to put us on good terms with them from the start.

We gave Mingma enough money to buy food and tea for the Sherpas for the time they should spend at, or below, base-camp, because they sensibly preferred their own food, rice, *dhal* and *atta*, to ours. They used our rations at higher altitudes, because they were more compact and more easily prepared on a mountain. During this time, they acquired a taste for certain items from our food which enlivened their own. Once a pot of jam disappeared with such astonishing rapidity that we inquired tactfully what had happened to it. " Oh! The Sherpas ate it," said Ang Temba with disarming frankness. But Mingma saw to it that we got plenty of potatoes and fresh eggs, in fair exchange.

Out of the sum we gave him, Mingma also bought a large pan like a preserving-pan for melting snow and cooking mountainous meals of rice, and cigarettes for the Sherpas. It is customary to allow them cigarettes, and no one went out of his way to tell us that only Bahu smoked.

We handed the Sherpas' equipment to them, for each was to carry his own, and they accepted what we gave them uncomplainingly, though Sherpas of other expeditions paraded in much smarter outfits before them in the bazaar. All our Sherpas except Kusung had climbing boots from previous expeditions better than the working men's hobnailers which were all we had been able to afford for them. They merely said with wry smiles, " We will wear our own, memsahib. They are better."

They were pleased with their air-mattresses, which were coloured red. We reflected that this would be highly appropriate if they should sell them to Communists afterwards, as was reported to be the practice. Their R.A.F. survival suits puzzled them, (and it is true that they looked

44

rather like an advertisement for Michelin tyres). They thought these were to be worn when climbing in extreme cold and could not understand why the feet were sewn up. When we explained they were meant to be sleeping-bags, they thought this was extremely funny and spent a long time zipping them up and down with much witty comment.

When all had been portioned out, we asked Mingma to let us see the hired ice-axes and crampons for the Sherpas, which we had arranged for him to bring from Darjeeling. Mingma looked blank and answered that he had not been given any. Monica said, " Oh! Christmas," and sat down on a kitbag. It was not her fault. We had been let down badly, for this arrangement was of long standing and quite definite. If we could not get hold of some we might as well not go at all, and these were not to be had in Kathmandu.

In the end this ironmongery, kindly lent from the store of the Himalayan Club in Calcutta, was rushed to us by air. It was rather a makeshift lot but we were thankful to see it emerge like plumbers' tools from the diplomatic bag in which it had been cunningly sent.

Our preparations complete, we went to exchange greetings with Raymond Lambert, who was soon to be our next-door neighbour in the Langtang. Of middle height, he wears specially built shoes, for all his toes have been amputated as a result of frostbite acquired in the Alps. He says he climbs better now, without them. He is a simple man with great personal magnetism, and can talk of himself and his plans without being in the least a bore.

" I am a good judge of character," he remarked. " After one climb with a man I know him inside out."

We thought he was impetuous and warm-hearted, and his charm was spoken of everywhere in Nepal. A little time-marking official in Raxaul who had talked with him

45

for a short while only, in the few words of English they had in common, was desolate that Raymond went home by another route, and was hardly consoled when we posed for him to take our photograph.

As we were leaving, a cocksure young man approached and announced himself as our liaison officer. We did not care for him much.

He said, " I would like to see the boots you have brought for me."

The fellow looked quite unfit for the march and likely to give trouble into the bargain. In Glasgow he would have worn a crew-cut and padded shoulders. He had no credentials and we suspected he was trying to foist himself upon us with the idea of telling the Deputy-Foreign-Secretary afterwards, " The ladies have chosen me." We said firmly, " There are no boots for you, but you are in for a lot of hard walking. Present yourself with your papers in the evening."

We never saw him again. Instead, a quiet lad, Murari Bahadur, turned up bearing a letter of introduction from the Government to the village authorities. He seemed about fifteen years old, though we later discovered he was a mature twenty, and he was so shy he would not look at us. We did not think he would show much initiative, in which we were mistaken, but on the other hand he did not seem likely to give trouble. He asked rather diffidently if he was going to be fed, but we did not hold that against him. We patted him on the back and told him to come in the morning with his bed-roll and some warm clothes.

We had a few hours left and went to see the ancient Bodnath temple, where Buddhists, our Sherpas among them, worship when in Kathmandu. It dates from the fifth century A.D. and has a great stupa, like an upturned pudding-basin, white except for the tower on top which is bricked with gold and painted with the all-seeing eyes of Buddha. The nose between is more disquieting to Western eyes, for it looks very like a question mark. There were prayer wheels round the foot and the carvings of some intruding Hindu deities and the whole was gaily festooned with prayer flags. The daughter of the presiding Chinni Lama showed us round. She was a very vivacious, modern young lady wearing spectacles with fancy-coloured frames.

She showed us the small side temple where butter lamps burn perpetually and told us about a young Frenchman who had been abusing the good Lama's hospitality under the pretence of being a student of the Tibetan language.

" He didn't like our cooking," she said. " He used to ask for dozens of eggs to make *crêpes suzettes*. It was supposed to be a treat for us, but he hadn't a clue about the recipe. And he actually had the nerve to be offended when we wouldn't eat them."

She took us upstairs to meet the Chinni Lama, saying confidentially, " Of course, Mummy and Daddy are quite eighteenth century," and entertained us to Tibetan butter tea, some strong liquor called arak and lots of scandal.

We had dinner on the last evening with Colonel Proud, First Secretary to the British Embassy, who was a delightful and amusing host. He told us that certain eminent climbers were in the habit of leaving tins of lice powder in the spare bedroom, an accident not always discovered before the next guest was installed. He loves the hills himself and was very kind to us, reassuring us for good and all about the people of Nepal, whom he said we should find courteous and friendly. This we found to be perfectly true. In general, some tribes of Western Nepal have a tradition of lawlessness in common with Tibet, and others are traders so sophisticated they do not give strangers a simple and hearty welcome. But in Central and Eastern Nepal everyone is naturally hospitable and the more drunk a man is, the politer he gets.

Assuring Colonel Proud that it was more important to us to return safely than to get to the top of any mountain, we hastened off to beat the 11 p.m. curfew. Monica pointed out that it would be novel to set out on a Himalayan expedition from the Kathmandu gaol, but Evelyn and I felt there would be enough novelty about our situation without that.

CHAPTER THREE

Over Himalayan Ridges

WE LEFT Kathmandu on 13th April. In spite of the inauspicious date and the fact that it was raining heavily that morning, we rose feeling cheerful and excited. The porters arrived at 7 a.m. with the Barianaik or labour contractor, who assured us that at the request of the Chief of Protocol he had chosen especially reliable men for us. They seemed a well set up, if somewhat ragged, crew. With them was their sirdar, and it appeared we had no choice but to take this man, though he informed us that he would not be carrying a load. He had a mournful face which, though it was sometimes transformed unexpectedly by a huge grin, gave us the impression that he was not cut out to be a leader of men.

More men came to offer their services than we had arranged to take on and this was fortunate, because, juggle as we would with the gear, it now divided into 31 loads, including the liaison officer's kit and the money-box, which were both heavier than we had bargained for. Evelyn, whose arithmetic runs along more conventional lines than either Monica's or mine, took the men's thumb-prints and gave them the customary advance. Rather surprisingly there was no squabbling and no surreptitious changing of loads among them.

They looked blank when we mentioned Tempathang.

49

Then we tried " Panch Pokhari ", the name of a place of
pilgrimage some miles west of Tempathang.

" Yes," they said with broad smiles. " Yes, we know the
way to Panch Pokhari." If we had had more experience of
Nepalis we would have known that this merely meant that
they had heard of it. Meanwhile we were reassured, and
the rain had ceased.

To make up for the day lost over the ice-axes and crampons, we had decided to go by lorry to Sankhu, eight miles
from Kathmandu, where the rough road peters out, to be
succeeded by many footpaths. The lorry now arrived, and
by dint of careful manipulation the porters managed to
squeeze themselves and their loads on board. When this was
done there was not room for a tin-opener more, and it must
have been quite impossible for anybody to scratch himself.

We followed in the jeep once we had got clear of the
reporters. There had been too much talk of conquering
peaks already and we were afraid of a further unseemly
splash in the press, which would make us look very foolish
if we never even got into the Jugal Himal at all. We kept
insisting that we were only going to explore a new area,
but they would not listen and repeatedly asked us, " What
is the name of that peak you are going to climb? "

" Will you camp at Sankhu to-night? " added one.

" Certainly not," I replied, indignant at the assumption,
for we should reach Sankhu at about 11 a.m., with most of
the day still ahead of us.

But this turned out to be a strategic error for, having thus
discovered that they would not be able to photograph us
at Sankhu later in the day, the reporters followed us at
once. We chased after the lorry and they chased after us
and, though nobody could go at more than 40 miles an
hour, it was quite as exciting as a gangster film, because of
the holes, ruts and chickens in the road.

The lorry, when we caught up with it, was an alarming sight. It was swaying so far at every lurch, it seemed likely that the men on the lower side would be able to look right under the lorry to the view beyond. After one particularly sickening jolt it stopped. The driver got out and ostentatiously examined the chassis, which turned out to have broken. He shook his head at the damage and looked reproachfully at the men packed sardine-wise on top. To

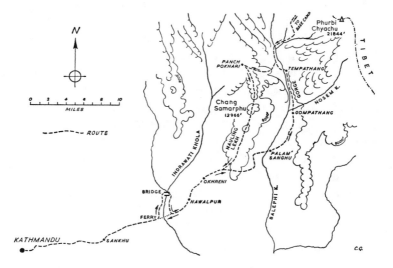

our surprise he then started up again. After all this by-play we decided that the chassis must have been broken before we started. We gave the man an extra 20 Nepali rupees (less than £1) as compensation, and he went away satisfied.

There was no hope of escaping quietly from Sankhu, for in two minutes an excited crowd was milling round us, peering into the jeep and trying to figure in every photograph we took. I found a stray hand in my pocket, which luckily contained nothing but Kirby-grips at the time. The Barahakim came out importantly, obviously saying in Nepali, " Now then, now then, what's all this? "

Murari surprised us by taking command of the situation, and stepped forward with our letter of introduction to explain that we were there by permission of the Government of Nepal and must be given every assistance. He prevented the important document from being passed round from hand to hand and stood over the Barahakim while he copied out the details laboriously.

" Three women? " this fellow seemed to be saying in a puzzled way, as if we were not standing there before him. " To the Jugal Himal, did you say? "

At last he was satisfied and salaamed in a friendly way. We went through an archway beyond the cobbled street of the Sankhu bazaar, and out into the open country. We were so taken up with our new impressions that it did not even occur to us that we had now left newspapers, telephones and wireless behind for a couple of months or so. Nor did we wish to hasten back to these amenities of modern life. In fact, when asked on our return what we thought of the Election results, we replied, " What Election? " with a regrettable lack of interest.

At first we went at a merry pace, but as midday approached every patch of shade and every beer shop was a lure no porter could resist—not to mention the chautaras. Chautaras are walls so built that a porter comes to rest by them with his bottom on a seat and his load on a parapet above. Our porters felt such a respect for the donors of these chautaras that they could not see their way to missing any of them out, even when going downhill.

In trying to keep with them and to keep them all together, we felt that we showed ourselves to be mere beginners at the game. We came to the conclusion that the old hand would probably stroll ahead and, having made sure that his home comforts were with the speediest of the porters, would enjoy the best of each succeeding day in camp. But there are tracks everywhere in Nepal, and as it was not always clear from our map which one we should take, we had to stay with the porters. All the tracks looked very much the same, thickly covered with glittering dust and patterned everywhere by the naked splay-toed feet of their users. We soon found that a porter who could not be seen for the dust was not necessarily going at top speed. It was of course their sirdar's duty to keep the porters moving, but he jogged along carrying a lantern only, and regarding the view like the man of leisure he was. Sometimes he stayed behind with the loiterers but on these occasions he seemed to be commiserating with them, rather than exhorting them to take up their loads and press on. In a day or so the men settled down to a steadier pace, and they were always ready to set off by 7 a.m. and willing to go on till 4 p.m. or even 5 p.m. if necessary.

Mingma sought an opportunity early in the day to talk to Monica and inquire respectfully about the life history of each one of us. All he gleaned was retailed to the other Sherpas—details of our way of life, our families and what we did for a living. They were especially interested in Monica's children and loved to see the photographs of them when, in a nostalgic mood, she brought them out. Mingma asked for our names, but found these so difficult to pronounce because of a speech defect he had, that in the end all he could manage was " Betty Memsahib " and " Evelyn Memsahib." The Sherpas used these names all the time and Monica was " the little Memsahib", though sometimes she was allowed to have a surname.

At first we passed through prosperous-looking country, where the houses were of a handsome brick, decorated with carved sills and lintels and with pots of flowers at the windows. The children looked healthy and were well dressed. But in spite of this the women filled their water-pots and washed their clothes at a stream which conveniently formed the main drain as well.

Beyond this we followed a woodland track to a watershed at about 6,000 feet, from which we could see all the surrounding countryside. Far below us was the Indrawati river, which we were to cross the next day. The hills ran in long, rounded spurs, brown and green, folding in upon one another and fading to purple as they receded. They were everywhere cultivated, and everywhere terraced, to prevent erosion in the monsoon—tier cut above tier for thousands of feet by the labour of centuries. Only the top of the watershed where we stood seemed to have escaped this infinitely patient carving, but even this had a trim look about it, like a park.

Here we brought out the map and had a lengthy consultation with Mingma and with the passers-by who stopped and crowded round to join in. We had spotted a long line of hills running north and slightly east, which we identified as the Nauling Lekh. They were linked by a high ridge which was over 10,000 feet throughout most of its length, and which culminated in Chang Samarphu, a hill almost 13,000 feet in height. The Nauling Lekh leads straight to Panch Pokhari, a holy place of five lakes above Tempathang, and it was this ridge we wanted to follow, by a pilgrim's path marked on the map. After the initial climb this route would be cooler than one through the valleys below and would give delightful high-level walking, which would help us to acclimatise and afford us a wonderful panoramic view of the Jugal Himal itself, thus helping us to plan our penetration of the area. There were snags, however. On such ridges as the Nauling Lekh water was likely to be scarce at this time of year. On the map the words, " Annual Fair, July," were printed beside Panch Pokhari. The pilgrims would use the path only at the time of this festival, which occurs during the monsoon, when they might acquire merit among the leeches and in the mud, and incidentally find water.

We could see snow, however, still lying on the higher tops. If we could reach this snow before making camp our problem of finding water would be solved. On the other hand, Mingma pointed out that the porters could not be expected to carry over snow in their bare feet. If the snow should melt before we got there the porters would be willing to go that way. But what then of our water supply? We seemed to have reached a deadlock.

At about 4 p.m. Mingma suggested making camp on the outskirts of a village. This did not appeal to us at all. In such well-populated countryside we had of course to insist that all our water should be boiled, wherever we camped, but there was no point in choosing a site on the very doorsteps of interested spectators. Even beyond the village we had difficulty in finding an uncultivated spot, and looked hopefully at a little mound covered with rough grass and scrub, but there were Hindu shrines on top, so we could not use that. Eventually we found some turf-covered terraces, each one wide enough to take a tent. This suited everyone, for the spectators got a good view from the terraces above us, as at a football match, and we had elbow-room below.

The three of us slept in Evelyn's Palomine, an already much-travelled tent, and the Sherpas used the Bungalow, which is a ridge tent and very roomy. They were rightly pleased to be given this and could hardly wait to blow up their air-beds. Perceiving this, we immediately decided that air-beds were essential to our comfort also, though

55

we had intended them to be solely for use on ice and snow.

The air-beds were Chhepala's job as a rule, and he wasted no lung-power over them, but learnt how to use the inflator at once by studying the pictures in our instruction book. Ang Temba was the table-waiter and filled this role with such aplomb, wearing the dish-towel over his arm as if it were a snow-white napkin, that at times we half expected him to produce a wine list. The medical chest, with a red-and-white checked cover, which afterwards replaced various Sherpa cloths of doubtful origin as the dish-towel, was ceremoniously arranged as our table and three food boxes as our chairs.

No sooner was all this set up to our satisfaction and the water inspected to see that it was really boiling, than a black thunderstorm came up. Lightning darted about the sky, the thunder roaring after it, and the rain drummed on our tents. The villagers fled, and the porters after them, no doubt to some more substantial shelter than our own. Mingma ran from tent to tent with my big black second-hand umbrella, which was never afterwards treated with the contempt it had at first aroused, and Kusung worked hard at digging draining-trenches, at the risk of blunting his axe. But the tents did not leak, and the storm did not keep us awake for long.

In the morning the air was sharp and clear. We came out to see the shapely hills stretching northward, their planes receding into the blue distance. Our eyes, accustomed to Scottish scenery, at first saw the faint white line above them as morning mist or cloud. It was only when we looked a second time that we realised with wonder and delight that the whole horizon from east to west was clasped by the Great Himalayan Chain. It is one thing to know from the map that there are mountains of this size in such numbers,

56

but it is quite another to see for oneself their beauty and awesome architecture, each one retaining its individuality in a bewildering profusion of peaks.

At 7 a.m. we were packed and ready and set off, dropping down to a tributary of the Indrawati where the terraces already showed the vivid green of sprouting grain, and where single trees, banyans and peepul grew to a magnificent size. Here we found a little water-mill grinding maize. The proprietor showed it off to us and then asked for a cigarette, managing to convey by his manner that he was not cadging but cementing a friendship. The tracks were busy and most of the passers-by carried loads. The wealthier sort had shoes, though as often as not they carried them. We were amused by the " double-take " most of them performed, looking back at us again when they realised that we were not something they met every day. The farther we marched, the fewer the people who were used to seeing Europeans, though even in Kathmandu we passed a man who was so interested in us that he fell off his bicycle.

" Are they men or women? " they would say among themselves, or to one of our porters, for Evelyn and I are taller than the average Nepali men and we all wore jeans on the march.

At about 9 a.m. we reached the Indrawati, a shrunken stream at this time of year, in a wide bed of bleaching sand and boulders. But even so it was a river to be reckoned with, husbanding its strength in a deep, swift central channel about fifty yards across. There was a ferry marked on the map but this did not necessarily mean that it still existed, and Murari, at our request, made inquiries about crossing the river at the first village we reached on its banks. He was told that the ferry was in fact in operation nearby. Unfortunately Mingma, who was some way ahead, did not know about the ferry and asked about a bridge. He was told there was one upstream and set off at a tremendous pace, going much too far ahead for us to call to him. We set off in hot pursuit along a path which followed a bluff above the river, climbing up and down in a maddening way. When at last Monica caught him up, he was about two miles beyond the ferry, and said the bridge he was looking for must be just around the corner. We were doubtful of the existence of this bridge, which was not marked on the map, but decided crossly that it would be better to go on a bit and see than to go back. Sure enough, less than a mile farther on we came to the bridge. But, having crossed it, we found there was no direct path on the far side to Nawalpur, the village where we had planned to make our next camp. We should have to walk right back along the far side of the Indrawati, bearing the heat and burden of the day, almost to the opposite side of the ferry again, before we could strike the path we wanted. The detour had cost us at least five miles.

Monica chose a moment when none of the other Sherpas was within hearing, to take Mingma quietly to task for rushing on ahead without consulting us, and to remind him that we had the map. He was apologetic and a little crestfallen.

"These Nepalis said they knew the way. Now they cannot find it after all," he said, deftly shifting the blame. We were amused to find that he did not think of himself as a Nepali, nor regard the porters as his countrymen.

We were now too limp in the heat of the enclosed valley to be bad-tempered and too dehydrated to be able to eat. We had filled our bottles with boiled water in the morning, but a mouthful now and then merely aggravated a thirst as consuming as ours. I gazed with longing at the river and at the porters scooping up water in their greasy black hats and tossing it down their throats, and argued that surely people had been known to drink such water and not die of typhoid. Our abstinence, I said, showed a lack of faith in providence and injections. But Monica, who had experience of the East, and Evelyn, who knew her tropical diseases, would have none of this.

We asked everyone we met how far it was to Nawalpur. But like the Highlander, they wished only to oblige with a pleasing answer, and no matter how far we travelled, they still said encouragingly, " ek kos," (two miles), except for one, more surly than the rest, who mentioned eight miles and nearly caused a sit-down strike by his frankness.

When we reached it, the path to Nawalpur rose steeply from the Indrawati, following a deep channel worn in the red earthen slopes by centuries of use and by monsoon flood, and at present cracked, dry, and sore on the eyes. Now, when we inquired of the people we met for Nawalpur, their voices rose in answer to a mere squeak (their way of expressing any extreme), as if they could hardly do justice to how much farther and higher up it was. Our resolution weakened. Moreover, it was now 4 p.m., and some of the porters were still far behind. We decided to call it a day.

Our men wanted to settle for the first camp-site the locals suggested where the water supply oozed from black mud much trampled by cattle. But hot and tired as we were, we rejected this out of hand, and both Monica and Murari cast about in search of running water. (It seemed ironical that we had thought so much about the dangers of flood during the months of preparation, only to meet with drought.) Eventually they found a nullah containing a trickle of water running over a leaf contrived as a spout. Above the nullah was some fallow ground cut out into broad terraces, and here we made camp.

As soon as the water was boiled we drank orange juice, then tea, then soup, then more tea. (Except for Evelyn who mystified the Sherpas by not liking tea, and stuck to orange juice. Tea is the staff of life to Sherpas.) We made up our minds never to suffer in this way again and hunted out the water-sterilising tablets, white and blue, which, if used in the right order and with the proper incantations, should make the water from streams safe to drink.

Again the local people gathered above us, though one or two children discovered that it was better fun to peep at us from below, in the hope of being chased. The landowner himself was there, regarding us benevolently. We had not asked his permission to camp, not knowing where to find him, but he seemed delighted with our trespass.

For the first time people came for medical attention prompted by one of the porters, whom Evelyn had treated for a boil on his cheek. She questioned them through Murari, who tried to line them up, with little success, as there is no such thing as a queue in Nepal. One poor old woman, almost blind with cataract of both eyes, came in the morning when we were about to leave. Evelyn explained sadly that she could do nothing to help, for she did not want to give eye-drops by way of consolation and so raise hopes which would not be fulfilled.

" Perhaps you will help me when you come this way again," said the old lady pathetically.

We were all a little disappointed at not having reached Nawalpur on the day we had planned to do so, but we were beginning to realise that patience was the first lesson to be learned at the feet of the Himalaya, and the sooner we got it over the better.

CHAPTER FOUR

Fire in the Gorges

OUR LIVES had now slipped into a primitive routine. We rose as soon as it was light—at about 5 a.m.—and went to bed when it was dark—about 7 p.m. More strictly speaking, I rose as soon as it was light and went about making brose, and emanating reproach, until the others felt they had to emerge from their sleeping-bags. In fact, I did enough early rising on this expedition to enable me to lie late and still keep a reputation for enthusiasm for the rest of my climbing life. Evelyn always resisted the pressure until the last possible moment, with the result that one morning the tent was suddenly invaded by enthusiastic Sherpas who brought it down about her ears as she struggled with the last stubborn trouser-zip.

In spite of our personal idiosyncrasies, we were finding that we got on well together, which was a good thing, as there is not much room for disagreement in a tent. Monica was much more relaxed than usual in our present surroundings. Her insight and quickness to see the funny side of a situation made her a most agreeable companion. Nothing troubled Evelyn unduly. Uncomplicated and easy-going, she never took offence. As for me, I generally mind far too much about what other people think. But in the Himalaya it did not seem worth while to worry over anything, even day-to-day problems as they arose.

It took us one and a half hours to reach Nawalpur, so we did not regret our decision of the night before not to press on. We had to spend some time there buying rice, for we were informed that Nawalpur was the last village we should find on our route big enough to have a bazaar, and forty people cannot live off the land if there is only a limited amount of grain to be had. We left the bargaining to Mingma because we knew we could trust him and also that we would get the rice more cheaply so than if we had bought it ourselves. Meantime we sat listening to the familiar notes of the cuckoo, sounding out of place in this arid region, and to a bird which Monica told us was a green barbet.

There were a number of small shops in the bazaar, each with carved wooden posts as its shop-front. The owners sat cross-legged on the floor among their merchandise, with everything to hand—chillies and spices all mixed up with cheap cigarettes, bracelets and plastic hair-clasps of the chain-store variety. Most of these shops had a brass water-pot with a long spout sitting on the threshold so that the passer-by might drink his fill. It was better than a dividend for attracting custom. One shop had a 1950 advertisement calendar proudly hung out as a trophy. Some of the houses in the village had shutters, on which were chalked the all-seeing eyes of Buddha. But there was also a shrine to Ganesh, the elephant god of the Hindus, at the cross-roads, indicating a commendable tolerance—or a desire to leave no deity unpropitiated.

We had to leave the rice in Nawalpur till we found extra porters to carry it, since it weighed four maunds (320 lb.). Mingma had heard that there was a Sherpa village called Okhreni some way above us and counted on getting extra men there, not in Nawalpur.

" These people," he said contemptuously, waving his

arm at a group playing with dice on a cloth chequer-board, and including all non-Sherpas, " These men cannot carry."

A little Sherpa girl from Okhreni offered to guide us to a maidan (a flat meadow) near her village, where we might camp. She made us walk in front of her and was delighted when we took the wrong path and gave her the opportunity to chivy us back to the right one. The countryside now changed markedly. The slopes of the Nauling Lekh rose immediately above us, covered at first by small wiry trees, interspersed with bald patches, and higher up by evergreen forest. Round Okhreni itself were a few maize and potato fields, but the rest was grazing land. The houses, too, were different—very like Swiss chalets in design. They had the same kind of roof, and were made of wood, covered on their lower half with mud-plaster painted white. This was real Buddhist country, and we saw the first *chortens* and a newly built prayer-wall. The people seemed more uninhibited here and the women bolder.

Murari always walked with us, though whether for our protection, which was quite unnecessary, or for his own prestige we did not know. He was a conscientious lad and probably felt he should be at hand to collect the things Monica left behind at every halt. He told us he was one of a family of seven, and that his father ran the only travel agency in Nepal. But as Nepalis very sensibly stay at home as a rule, his business was not a flourishing one, and he found it difficult to provide for his family and their education.

We discovered that when the people asked Murari where he came from he always said " Nepal," as if we were not in Nepal already. This added greatly to our feeling of unreality. But he explained that old Nepal was the valley of Kathmandu. These people still thought of Nepal thus, and of themselves as " paharis," or hill-men.

63

Tents in the Clouds

We reached the grassy maidan early in the day, at about
2 p.m., having covered only six miles. Usually we did
about ten miles each day, but we could go no farther until
our arrangements for the rice were completed. Mingma
worked hard, as if to make amends for his mistake of the
day before. He persuaded two Sherpa lads from Okhreni
to come with us as porters, and another two to follow later.
With some of the old hands he twice made the journey to
Nawalpur and back, fetching up the rice. He packed as
much of it as possible into four loads and distributed the
remaining rice among the Kathmandu porters. He did
not return from the last of his negotiations until late at
night, so we concluded that they had been wound up over
a jar of *chang* (the village beer).

Rather to our disappointment we found that we did not
like either *chang* or *rakshi*, a raw spirit brewed from rice.
Our mistake with the *rakshi* was in sipping it. The stuff
should be knocked back. *Chang* is not so bad if sipped
through a bamboo straw from a closed jar. Otherwise the
sight of it is very off-putting, for it looks like disinfectant,
though by no means so hygienic.

We were quite happy to spend the afternoon on our
maidan, which was a grass shelf below the crest of a hill,
enclosed on three sides by jungle and open on the fourth
to a splendid array of mountains, which we identified as the
Jugal Himal and the Langtang Himal. We could see the
ridge of the Nauling Lekh rising gently to Chang Samarphu
with its small push-button of a top, and we could see the
last of the snow melting before our eyes. But tall trees,
rhododendron and conifer, stood along its entire length,
and carried away by our enthusiasm, we reasoned that
where there are trees there must be water. Mingma, as
anxious as we were to follow this route, succeeded in getting
one of the Okhreni youths to say he knew where to find

64

water on the ridge, but the porters were not convinced. In the evening it became delightfully cool, for we were now at 7,500 feet and a light wind blew straight from the eternal snows. Our minds were made up to stay high, unless this was proved impossible.

Meanwhile, I decided to make a steamed pudding as a special treat. It has been said that cooks in the Himalaya should not be allowed to languish from faint praise. I was not given any praise at all. My friends said that, as far as they were concerned, there were not going to be any more puddings. The whole thing was a great joke with the Sherpas, and I had to bury the remains so as not to admit my failure.

Murari always joined us at our meals, turning his back slightly so as not to watch us eating. At first he would never help himself and even when food was pressed on him ate little for a lad of his years . . . compared with Ang Temba, for instance, who could put away huge platefuls of rice at every sitting. Murari was proving a good walker, but how long would he be able to keep this up on so slender a diet? Later this afternoon, however, he retired to his tent and shortly afterwards we saw Mingma slip one of those same huge platefuls of rice after him. Further observation showed that Murari accounted for more calories per day than anyone else in the party. When he became less shy he made no secret of eating both our food and the Sherpas', thus making the best of both worlds.

Next morning, while the porter's sirdar was warming his back sorrowfully at the fire, leaving Murari and our Sherpas to help his porters to rise to their feet with their loads, a sharp altercation arose. One of the porters claimed that his load had been unfairly increased. I was collecting a vocabulary of useful Nepali terms and it suddenly occurred to me that I did not know the word for " heavy." Murari gave it to me, and, oblivious to the quarrel now developing, I practiced it. " *Garhun*," I said loudly, " *Garhun* " over and over again to get the pronunciation right. " Yes, memsahib, *garhun*," said the dissatisfied porter, turning to me. And as if it were enough that his grievance had been recognised he slung on his headband, clapped his little black hat on top, and made off.

It was not easy to learn Nepali because there were so many other languages in the party. The porters spoke a dialect called Tamang, the Sherpas had their own tongue and the villagers we met before we reached Sherpa territory spoke Newari, a language quite unlike Nepali. Most of our men had a smattering of Hindustani and spoke Nepali as a common language. I was always so overjoyed when I recognised a word in the babel around me, that I had to go and tell someone about it.

The porters went very slowly that day and stopped more often than usual to ease their loads or to expectorate with great deliberation. (The sound of this was always with us, but I used to console myself by thinking that some Saturday night, hearing it on a Glasgow tramcar, I would think with nostalgia of Nepal.) They would not hurry for Mingma's shouts of " Pep, pep! Lo, lo! " nor at their sirdar's command. Nor did they whistle and sing in their usual way. We never shouted at them ourselves but to-day Evelyn walked at the back of the line, waiting pointedly for those who rested too long. This method had some success. Only once that day did we see a porter galvanised into action with his load, and that was not to anyone's order, but in answer to a gay little quip from Ang Droma as she skipped past with her own. The general reluctance to keep moving was caused by their uneasiness over the Nauling Lekh route.

Monica and I went ahead with Murari, hoping this would encourage the porters, and at about 8,000 feet stopped to speak with some hill-men, descending with loads of close-packed leafy branches, fodder for their cattle.

"Yes," they said to us, "there is a spring up there." Their voices in describing its distance from and height above us rose characteristically to such a pitch, that I was afraid to bring the Jugal into the conversation at all in case any of them should permanently damage his larynx. We waited for the porters, hoping that the latest information would reassure them. But quite the reverse. . . . When our informants saw the size of our retinue they retracted, saying their spring was too small. We should have to march for three days along the Nauling Lekh, they said, before finding enough water for so many people. If we did not believe them, all right, we could go and see for ourselves.

This caused an outcry. The porters crowded round Monica, pleading and expostulating.

"We shall all die up there, memsahib," said one dramatically.

"No you won't," was the prosaic reply. "If there is no water higher up we shall go by the lower path, that's all."

We were disappointed, particularly as we could now see what we thought was the alternative—a path which descended hearty-breakingly towards the Indrawati again on the west side of the Nauling Lekh, to contour endlessly among the mosquitoes and villages. But to our surprise, one of the new Sherpa porters now indicated that we should follow yet another path, dropping down east of the Nauling Lekh to the Balephi Khola. On our map this path stopped some miles short of Tempathang, where the river emerged from a deep gorge. We had not even considered following it. We expected to have to force our way through gorges enough, without deliberately and unnecessarily seeking out another. But the Sherpa boy assured us that this path continued all the way to Tempathang, and he made it sound like an arterial road.

" It's wide enough to take a yak, memsahib ! " he exclaimed, as if he could say no fairer than that.

This path we took, and now everyone was happy—the porters because they were not going to die, Mingma because he could say to them, " All right, you've had your way, but no more stopping every five minutes," and the three of us because this was no depressing detour but a route which took us along the very river which flowed from the glaciers of the Jugal Himal itself.

We set off downhill at a smart pace, contouring the forested flanks of the Nauling Lekh and gradually descending towards the river. Many clear streams flashed across our path, which was a highway indeed, stone-flagged and shaded by rhododendron trees. But to our disappointment the red flowers had withered and were strewn along the path like the decorations after a party. Towards evening we found ourselves on a spur which descended very steeply to the Balephi Khola, and camped on a broad terrace some way down where a barn-like structure, open to travellers, gave the porters shelter for the night.

Our focus was now narrowed by the shaggy hillsides, steepening on either side of the river and articulating in its deep cleft below. Soon it would be impossible in this wild country to stray from the paths or to proceed any farther except by entering the gorges of the Balephi Khola. Beyond these gorges we could see the mountains of the Jugal. We lay for a long time with map, compass and binoculars, picking out Dorje Lakpa to the west and Phurbi Chyachu to the east, the only two mountains of the group which are named, probably because they lie farther south than the rest and are more prominent when seen from Kathmandu. Among ourselves we called them George and Phoebe.

Fire in the Gorges

From our viewpoint Dorje Lakpa looked the most striking of the whole group, and appeared to have two lovely slender tops. The name of the whole range may derive from this for " Jugal Himal " may mean " peak of twin summits.'

We were forced reluctantly to the conclusion that Tilman had been right in calling the Jugal Himal uncompromising. These mountains owed much of their beauty to the sharp pinnacles bright in the sun, the stupendous overhangs of snow and ice and the polished slopes, which made them appear completely impregnable. Between the two named peaks was another, probably higher and certainly farther away, which rose to a graceful summit. The angle of its ridges appeared to be gentler and, though its lower ramparts might well contrast sharply with this and present greater problems, it was for the moment an encouraging sight. As the light faded, reducing the patterns of the mountains to mere bulky shadows, grey as battleships, companionable fires shone out on the hillsides around us, and we returned to our own.

By this time we had shaken down comfortably as a party, and a kind of protocol had established itself. For instance, the porters' sirdar kept his end up by having no load, and by wearing a very smart pair of high-altitude boots, whose origin no doubt was an Everest expedition. Our Sherpas were the élite of hill-carriers, men from Sola Khombu, who did not need to parade in fancy boots on the march. Besides, they had proper mountaineers' rucksacks (though Chhepala carried his on a headband and no nonsense). Murari, who was a friendly unassuming lad, popular with all ranks, nevertheless underlined his position with a waterproof-covered topi and a pair of dark glasses which made him look very much the intellectual. We gave him the binoculars to carry, as a kind of insurance against their loss, but they were so very good for dignity that Mingma

69

collared them later on. It is only fair to add that when Mingma carried them he put them to frequent and practical use.

On our downward journey the next day we kept meeting people, some of them mere boys, travelling to Kathmandu with huge rectangular blocks of wood, cut in the forests higher up, tied on their backs. The path was so narrow and the slope so steep that in some places we had great difficulty in passing them.

This path led down to the Balephi and, though there was a continuation of it running along the true right bank of the river, our Sherpa guide indicated that we should cross by a big chain bridge to another path on the opposite side. The bridge was constructed of two rows of rough and narrow planks, more or less pegged together, with two chains for handrails, which were lightly connected to the planks. This contraption swayed alarmingly about fifty feet above the swift river and, if there were two or three people on it at once, it bounced up and down as well. The handle of my umbrella (known to my friends as " that umbrella ") kept catching in the links of the chain, usually just as a swirling green eddy below caught my eye. One of the porters took fright and would not cross with his load.

The village on the far side was called Palam Sanghu. Here, we were told, a lama runs the only school for many miles around. While the people looked at us and we in self-defence looked at the people, the Sherpas and porters slipped off in ones and twos to the *chang* shop, to congratulate themselves, no doubt, on a safe crossing. Mingma, between visits of his own, made rallying shouts. Chhepala went down to the river to wash and oil his long hair, leaving it spread over his shoulders till it dried. I noticed that some of the infants who were big enough to run about were still being breast-fed. The younger children went naked, except for one or two whose shirts were so ragged that they looked like floor-cloths hung out to dry. One mother snatched up her little pot-bellied boy and fled with him when we tried to photograph him. This surprised us for, as a rule, Nepalis love to be in front of a camera. These people were not Sherpas, who never live below about 7,500 feet, and their village, though picturesque, was dirty. Sherpa villages are clean.

The track along the true left bank of the Balephi was rough, and hard to follow. Sometimes it climbed high above the river to a village, and sometimes it twisted down and ran for a while over the white sand and pebbles of the river-bed. Monica had wrenched her knee and as it was more painful when going downhill this switchback travel was trying for her. I was hot, though I dipped my despised umbrella in every stream and carried it dripping over my head. Consequently we were both cross with Evelyn, when, inspired by Chhepala's example, she suddenly decided to wash her hair in the middle of a ford which the porters were about to cross and was caught by them with a magnificent head of shampoo. " Really, Evelyn, you might have chosen a less public place," we said sharply. But when she promised disarmingly to be more discreet another time we were mollified and planned to wash our own hair when a suitable time and place should present itself.

We camped that night among some boulders with a great tree above our tents, the stars shining in its branches like buds. A cloud of smoke had been drifting from slopes upstream all afternoon and, though we had paid little attention to it then, we now saw a glow spread in the sky, so vivid that it suggested the glow from a factory furnace rather than a burning hillside.

Next day we entered the narrow gorge which the Balephi has carved below Tempathang. On either side the hillsides, forested except where gaunt slabs and walls of rock intruded, plunged to the river, chafing among its rocks below. We had to prevent our eyes from straying to the dazzling heights of Dorje Lakpa above, or the precipitate descent of the ground below, for this was not the place for a false step. Across the slopes went a threadlike path, sometimes faintly marked, sometimes in well-placed rock steps. A few of the porters were hesitant on this terrain but none of them showed signs of wanting to turn back, for which we were thankful. But we began to wonder how they would manage to follow the Upper Balephi, where, according to the map and to Tilman's account of his visit to Tempathang, we could not expect to find any track at all, however vestigial, and might have to force our way through thickets, traverse ledges, and climb cliffs.

Rounding one steep corner, we came on a desolate scene. The fire manifested in the sky the day before had been here, and nothing remained but charred, truncated trees, blackened slopes, and ashes lying thick on the ground. As we crossed this stretch a single boulder, loosened by the fire, struck at us silently from above, with no ricochet to warn us. As it fell between Evelyn and Monica they saw burning turf clinging to it.

This was the first stretch of forest devastated by fire we came upon, but by no means the last. The local people burn the grass just before the monsoon to encourage new growth for the grazing of their animals, but as this is of course the driest season of the year, the fires often get out of control, valuable timber is lost and on steep slopes erosion is caused and the danger of landslides increased.

Hurrying to get away from this place, we came to a shelf of big boulders overlooking the Nosem Khola, a stream which drains the small south-eastern glaciers of the Jugal Himal and joins the Balephi Khola just below Tempathang.

Fire in the Gorges

Here the path turned sharply eastward and dropped to the Nosem Khola. But immediately before us, barring our way, was the forest fire itself, still alive, crackling among the trees and attended by a pall of smoke. Mingma went down to have a closer look at it and returning, gave it as his opinion that we should have to wait at least an hour before it would be safe to proceed. There was nothing for it but to sit down and try to be patient.

But Monica said, " Really I don't see why we shouldn't just go on. We have jungle fires in South India and you can walk right through them if you keep a sharp look-out."

No sooner had she said this than there was a tremendous roaring from the depths of the valley, and clouds of smoke puffed upward. For a moment we thought that another fire was coming straight at us from below, till we remembered that everything was already burnt where we stood. Suddenly we saw a great consuming sheet of flame leaping up the hillside opposite with the terrifying speed of an avalanche. It swept across the line we should have taken had we kept to the true right bank of the Balephi, and nothing in its path could have escaped.

A little shaken, we turned again to the fire ahead of us. But the jungle here was a mixture of deciduous trees and evergreen rain forest, more like the South Indian variety known to Monica, which would not flare up as dramatically as the inflammable mixture of dry conifer and dry bamboo on the other side. The wind seemed to be driving our fire slowly uphill. After the hour was over one of the Okhreni Sherpa boys went down to inspect it again. He came back and without a word took up his load and set off. We all followed as quickly as we could. The fire was still licking at the undergrowth and burning in the trees on either side of the path and the heat was great. We were anxious about Ang Droma's long skirt and about the bare-footed

73

porters, for we felt that our feet would soon be blistered, even through our gym shoes. But it was the back of Monica's shirt which went on fire and it was lucky that Murari noticed this and put it out in the nick of time. When we reached the far side of the burning stretch, Mingma and I tried to prevent the fire from spreading eastwards along the path until everyone was out of range, but as soon as we got it out in one place little tongues of flame would stick out at us in another, until we gave it up as a bad job.

By this time we were quite close to the Nosem Khola and made for it thankfully. We found a perfect camp-site on the near bank, where the air smelt sweet and clean and a bird was singing, which I actually identified as a flycatcher. Monica, Evelyn and I paused only to dump our rucksacks and grab our soap before going a good way upstream to a secluded pool to bathe and wash off the dust and ashes of the day. The water was icy, so that we could only rush in and out again with terrible cries, and when we washed our hair our heads became numb with cold.

CHAPTER FIVE

Tempathang — Threshold of the Jugal Himal

W<small>E WERE</small> now very near Tempathang—indeed if it had not been for the fire we might have reached it that night instead of camping by the Nosem Khola.

The following morning we crossed this river and climbed up again very steeply for about 2,000 feet by a path which was more like a ladder. The people of Nepal take their hills straight, and no gentle zigzags come between them and their determination to gain height.

The opposite sides of the valley were now so sheer and so close together they rose like the pages of a book about to shut. Here and there the slopes were broken by a tiny saucer of green, a yak-pasture or a potato field. No patch where the general angle eased went uncultivated. We saw a thickly wooded ridge on the far side, dropping from where we judged the five lakes of Panch Pokhari must be. Another uncompromising path from Panch Pokhari to Tempathang must follow this ridge.

A man without a load went past, grizzled and bent, with a long striped scarf like a football supporter's round his neck. He spoke to us in passing and Murari told us he was offering to find porters for us if we wanted them for the next stage of our march. We did not think he could realise we were bound for the mountains but guessed that he had been button-holed by Mingma, who was still some way behind.

Tempathang is a Sherpa village, rather less than 8,000 feet in height, and our Sherpas were eager to reach it and to meet their own kind. Mingma wanted to recruit new men there, hill folk who spoke his own language, and to have the Kathmandu porters, whom he regarded as no better than Sassenachs, sent home. (We ourselves had begun to call these porters " the Nepalis " as distinct from Sherpas, though of course Sherpas too, belong to Nepal.) He probably also wanted to have single authority, and to this end had even talked of recruiting yaks though, as the gorge narrowed and the track became more rudimentary, we heard less of this scheme.

As we approached the village, perched on slanting shelves above a steep drop to the river, he shot ahead with a " Sherpas wha' hae " look in his eye. We reached the first houses well before noon and found the place almost deserted. One very old man lay in the sun as if at death's door, a skinny arm across his face ; a few women were weaving long bamboo mats and a boy was combing out some wool. We came to the conclusion that all the able-bodied men were hiding from Mingma who was canvassing from door to door. When he returned, the only definite information he had was of a good camp-site down by the river beyond Tempathang. There was no hope of proceeding farther that day, for we had to find out as much as we could about the Jugal Himal from the local people, if possible securing one of them at least as a guide. We had also to arrange to leave food here against our return. But the camp-site itself was excuse enough to linger. On the banks of the river were rough grass and greenthorn trees and intermittent stretches of pale sand gleaming in the sun. A pair of white-capped redstarts hopped from stone to stone near us. We set up camp and sat on smooth white boulders with our feet in the river, mesmerised by its swift, graceful movement.

It was now 19th April. The first stage of our journey was completed—the fifty miles or so from Kathmandu to Tempathang. This we might have covered in five days instead of six and a half had it not been for the aggregation of small delays. Yet we no longer worried about time, the present was such pleasure. Nor did we worry overmuch about the problems immediately ahead.

Presently the old man in the long red and green scarf came down to speak to us. He seemed to be a man of some standing in the village, and his name, we later discovered, was Nima Lama. In answer to our eager questioning he said that there was a path following the Balephi Khola to some yak pastures higher up, and that the highest of these, three days' march beyond Tempathang, lay near a glacier. He himself, he said, had been up almost close enough to put his hand on the ice, and he would certainly come with us and show us the way.

We were highly elated. This was great news. It was in flat contradiction to what Tilman had been told. We came to the conclusion later that the explanation was not that the Tempathang people had recently changed their practice and gone back to using these high alps; more probably in 1949, they had reported on the track to them as adversely as they could, so as to discourage Tilman from going up during the monsoon. Then, indeed, tracks and bridges are washed away and they would not want to be talked into accompanying him.

Now that we knew there was a path we began to consider where it might lead.

77

On our map three main valleys were shown draining the Jugal Himal, running roughly parallel, north and south. The central and most easterly of these contained big glaciers.

Now, the maps of Nepal were made by enterprising Indian surveyors and though their scale is small—a quarter of an inch to the mile—they are reasonably accurate as far as the foothills are concerned. But we knew that the mountain ranges had been drawn from a respectful distance. Some of the peaks of the Jugal have been triangulated, probably from a ridge above and to the west of Tempathang, and there are in fact three main valleys, but apart from this the map of the area is largely guesswork.

Because we followed a low-level route on the march in, we were not able to glean much from our own observation, but we had decided that, assuming the map was correct in showing three main valleys, then the central one must lead to the high peak lying between Dorje Lakpa and Phurbi Chyachu which had taken our fancy. Only the upper structures of these mountains had been visible to us on the march, but even so this high peak was the only one we had seen so far that was likely to prove climbable, and we wanted to examine it at closer range. Of course our real aim was to explore, not to climb peaks, but the contours on the map indicated that this central glacier lay at an easy angle. If this were so it should form a highway to the heart of the Jugal itself. The western valley contained a series of smaller and probably disconnected glaciers, while the glacier in the third eastern-most valley was shown as much steeper than the central one—a more formidable proposition altogether. All things considered, the central glacier seemed to offer most possibilities and to be the one for us.

We could not determine which glacier Nima Lama's path led to. He said it lay between Phurbi Chyachu (which

78

he called Phurawa Chyachm, a version instantly adopted by our Sherpas) and Dorje Lakpa. It might therefore be the central glacier or the difficult eastern one. The sensible course, however, was to follow the old man's path in the first instance and to study the lie of the land on the way.

Nima Lama added that the path was rough and steep, and looked at the Nepali porters doubtfully as if sizing them up against the hazards he anticipated. Mingma got him to say this again in case we had not taken the point.

While we were still studying the map a minor crisis arose. Hearing of our attempts to raise Sherpa manpower, the porter's sirdar came and said that his men had contracted to go to base camp and that if some were sent back now, all would go back. Certainly none would carry loads alongside local amateurs. He became quite impassioned and to mark the climax of his peroration, spat.

This ultimatum complicated matters. We wanted to keep on some of the younger Nepalis, for Mingma had only succeeded in rounding up a dozen or so of the villagers at most. Even after depositing some food in Tempathang we would still need about 25 porters to come with us to base camp.

Privately we inclined to Mingma's plan, for the Tempathang men would have plenty of food for themselves, though their supplies would not stand the strain of feeding the Nepalis, who seemed likely to run short. Also if we took on the Tempathang men we need only keep one or two of them at base camp to fetch up others, instead of paying a squad of Nepalis to sit idle. But we warned Mingma that we would only dismiss the Nepalis if he could produce a full team of Sherpas, men or women, who would be prepared to return with us all the way to Kathmandu.

The Nepali porters left all the negotiations to their sirdar. They had fires going all round the camp, and in one group some younger men played an uproarious game, throwing stones at one another. The idea was to catch the stone, or if not, to dodge it, but we imagined it would be as much of a penalty to succeed in catching it as to be struck.

We found that both Mingma and the porters' sirdar were more reasonable in private than in open discussion, and the afternoon was pleasantly taken up with diplomacy and intrigue. Between interviews, Ang Temba brought us tea in the whistling kettle. This kettle was a great comfort to us, and to Monica in particular, for its whistle proclaimed the extinction of all indigenous germs. If he thought we had forgotten to listen for it, Ang Temba would shake the kettle as he brought it over, eliciting the last faint squeaks, and grinning, as if to say, " You see? Boiled! "

Ang Droma found a militant variety of stinging nettle which, she said, was good to eat. She cut down swatches of it with a kukri, stewed it, and then wrung out the mass of vegetable with her hands as if it were a dishcloth. The remains, fried in butter, were delicious.

The Sherpas spent the afternoon improving the camp-site. They always built excellent fires, kindled, however, with a liberal dose of paraffin, and dug trenches for draining, round the tents, even when the sky was clear. They loved to introduce new gadgets of their own invention and manufacture each day. One day they would cut down a branch, lop off its twigs and set it up as a stand on which they hooked the mugs. On another they would devise a washing-line from two branches placed upright and a long sapling slung between them. Our food boxes were appropriated as they fell vacant, to be made up into kitchen furniture, and Chhepela adopted a lid as a baking-board. When our Sherpas made chupattis, which are like potato scones made from coarse flour, they did not flip them from hand to hand in the traditional manner, but rolled them professionally on this board, with a rolling-pin contrived from a thick branch, carefully smoothed under a kukri blade. The only thing they were not good at in camp was pitching the tents, and this was because they pegged them too widely, spoiling the hang of the canvas. It was as if, from habit born of gregariousness, they wished to make room in each tent for as many people as possible. But in the preparation of a good bivouac—or to use the Scots word " howff "—they were unbeatable.

In the morning, Mingma proudly presented his new team of porters, at least twenty-five of them. They were a wild and ragged crew with unkempt hair and piratical mien, their kukris stuck arrogantly through their belts. They looked tough enough in all conscience, but some were mere boys and one was a cretin. Mingma explained that most of the men of the village had been away cutting wood in the forests above, but word had gone round of our arrival and these had come down to join the fun and hear of something to their advantage.

They seemed to be of mixed race, for not all had the Mongolian features of the Sola Khombu Sherpa. Like the Nepali porters, they went barefoot and wore loincloths and shirts which came down over their lean thighs. Some had short woollen coats, woven in their own homes, others Western-style pullovers from the Kathmandu bazaar, one of an astonishing purple hue. Nearly all of them wore coloured beads or earrings and the little black Nepali hats. One fellow had an ancient tooth-brush hanging from his necklace, another an A.F.S. button, which must have had a remarkable history.

We soon found that they were a simple people, but not entirely unsophisticated. Three or four times a year they go to Kathmandu to trade their *ghee* for rice, and the clothes they cannot produce themselves. When we returned to the city with them, we found that their only reaction to a motor-car was to hoot back derisively, expressing very much what we felt ourselves.

Mingma told us these men were asking seven " mors " a day. Thinking " mor " was Sherpa for " rupee," we were aghast and nearly dismissed them on the spot. But it transpired that a mor is half a rupee and they were asking only what we paid to the Nepali porters. We gave in with pretended reluctance.

We soon made friends with our Sherpa porters. They were well disposed to us from the beginning, for they are a naturally hospitable people and no doubt they found us good entertainment. The friendship was sealed over the medical chest, and with gifts of empty tins. Tins are practically currency in Nepal, and any we disposed of were seized at once, to reappear, often still unwashed, as dice-boxes or *chang* jars. Sometimes one of the younger boys would hang about our tents forlornly just when he thought we were about to polish off the last of the jam, say, and thus empty another tin. Usually our hearts were touched, and the manœuvre succeeded. Even cardboard cartons were scrutinised for their usefulness and the children fought tooth and nail for scraps of coloured paper.

They all loved the medical chest and would stand for hours breathing over its gaily coloured contents and trumping up symptoms to prolong the session. One, more original than the rest, thought of enlisting Evelyn's sympathy for hacks on the leathery soles of his feet. The black tar ointment she gave him so fascinated the onlookers, that sore feet became the popular ailment.

Some were genuinely ill, like the poor old man we had seen the day before, who was mere skin and bone and very weak from dysentery. He was Evelyn's most satisfactory case, for she treated him with sulfa drugs and word came up later that he had been completely cured and wanted some more wonder-working pills. Sulfa drugs are dangerous if irresponsibly taken, however, and she sent vitamin pills instead. These were bright orange and were even more enthusiastically received.

Others had tuberculosis in varying forms, mostly bovine in origin. Eye troubles were the most common and a number of people suffered from partial blindness due to old scar tissue on the cornea.

We got rid of as much coin as possible in paying off the Nepalis for it turned out that paper money of small denominations was acceptable in Tempathang after all. We found that Nepalis do not mind how much their employer bargains with them, as we now did over the number of days' pay due for the return march, so long as they get their baksheesh, even though it may come to the same thing in the end. We gave the Nepali sirdar the chit he asked for, to show we were satisfied with him and his men, and the last letters home. They went off singing, glad to turn their backs on inhospitable country.

Signing on the Tempathang men was rather like getting up a party. They all crowded round eager to give their names and thumb-prints. They were presided over by their spokesman, a small hunched man in a jacket green with age, whose straight hair stuck out round his hat like a chimney sweep's brush. Because of this we called him Simple Simon, but he was far from simple, being in fact something of a wag. His real name was Tensing Lama.

We turned away one lad who could not have been quite twelve years old, but he kept coming back in the hope that we would think he was someone else, for he did not want to be left behind with the women-folk. We were on the point of rejecting another, not much older, but his father said he would come up and relieve the boy next day. He could not come himself at once, for one of his yaks had just died and the meat would have to be smoked for later use.

In Buddhist country it is considered wrong to take any animal's life. Stricter Buddhists will not eat the flesh even of an animal which has died a natural death. But these Sherpas were not orthodox, a fact borne in on us in the ensuing weeks, when we were forced to retire from a perfectly good camp-fire by the smell of this same yak's meat stewing.

Finally, with Mingma beaming all over his face, now that he had his Sherpa porters, we set off upstream by a path which was here and there indistinct, into a country where no white person had preceded us.

CHAPTER SIX

The One Way to the Glaciers

For a time the path kept to the bed of the stream, taking us northwards. Through the trees we could see the glacier water, like green milk, pouring between boulders and gathering force in slowly swirling pools.

Monica's knee was troubling her again and in case we should be left behind, Nima Lama appointed himself our guide, a lantern slung symbolically on his load, and walked with the three of us and Murari. We began to follow his custom of dropping leaves by the prayer-flag at the top of each steep slope, in thank-offering for having surmounted it.

Tensing Lama on the other hand decided he was sirdar, though he did not attempt to control the others or behave in any way differently from them. There was no nonsense, however, about his being paid extra or walking unloaded, so we did not object to the appointment.

It was evident that the Tempathang men considered this journey to the mountains as something of a jaunt and did not intend to spoil the holiday atmosphere by taking things too seriously, or hurrying, for instance. At first we wondered if we had dismissed a disciplined band of professional porters with reputations to consider, only to find them replaced by irresponsible, if likeable, rapscallions.

They walked faster than the Nepalis—they could run with their loads without any trouble—but they stopped

85

often to enjoy life and consider the next stage. Soon, instead of being guided from the rear, we found ourselves forging ahead.

This erratic progression was, as Monica pointed out, typical of Tibetan peoples, and no doubt these independent Sherpas came of Tibetan stock. Nagging and exhortation were useless. As they saw it, they had contracted to get us to a specified place in three days and they would keep to the bargain if left to do it in their own way. If we had offered them three days' pay to get us up in two, they would not have been interested nor changed their programme in the least.

At one halt we asked them about a tiny hamlet, Mahatan, wrongly shown on our map as well north of Tempathang, but we called it " Matahan " by mistake. This was greeted with uproarious mirth and our mispronunciation was imitated and others invented, each play on the word being funnier than the last. It was afterwards quite impossible to have the subject discussed with any degree of sobriety.

Towards midday Nima Lama indicated that we would have to cross the main river and follow a side-stream joining it from the east.

The name " Balephi Khola " is used by the local people as a comprehensive term for a network of streams. There are three main branches approximately marked on the map, draining the three main glacier valleys. Where we now stood the Langtang Khola, flowing south from the peaks bordering the Langtang Himal and the small glaciers of the westernmost valley, was joined by the Pulmutang Khola. The Pulmutang Khola flows from the easternmost valley and drains the glaciers of Phurbi Chyachu. Between them the Rakhta Khola flows roughly south-west to join the Pulmutang from the central glacier, the main Dorje Lakpa glacier, which we were so anxious to reach. It was therefore the Rakhta Khola we wanted to follow.

We had not travelled more than four miles from base camp and I did not think we could have reached the junction between the Langtang Khola and the Pulmutang Khola yet, for it was shown on the map much farther from Tempathang. I complained that we were being sidetracked along a small tributary, which would lead us to the lesser hills south of the main range. But as I warmed to my theme Evelyn slipped down to investigate and found that this new stream was a glacier stream after all, thick with white sediment. It could only be the Pulmutang Khola.

North of the junction the course of the Langtang became a gorge, walled up completely along its true right bank, the slopes on the left being very steep and forested. Nima Lama affirmed that there was no path through this gorge and that no one ever went up the Langtang Khola. It was the Langtang on which Tilman in 1949 had looked down from above. Our path climbed the shoulder now facing us on the far side of the Langtang till high above the junction of the rivers, and according to Nima Lama there was a camping-place hidden from us, and about 1,000 feet above us. We decided to set up camp there and in the afternoon to round this shoulder northwards, and try to force a way up the true left bank of the Langtang Khola. This was fortunate, for the porters, too, had decided to stop for the day.

We crossed the Langtang by a solid, well-maintained bridge of logs. On the near-vertical sections of the path above, tree-trunks were placed upright as ladders, holds hewn out in them for hands and feet. We came out on a grassy meadow, from which we could see the blunt white head of Phurbi Chyachu dominating the eastward-running valley of the Pulmutang which we should enter next day. A few huts skirted potato fields, overlooked by a tiny locked *gompa*, some formidable Buddhist devils sporting themselves in garish colours on the front wall. We asked if we might enter but the porter told us the lama was away and his mother-in-law had the key—as much as to say, that was that. Beyond were pleasant lawns, surrounded by briars and rhododendron trees in full bloom. We might have been in the policies of a well-kept estate. So much, so far, for the impassable gorges of the Jugal Himal.

The picture was quite different to the north. The three of us set off, rounding the shoulder, till we were again above the junction of the rivers. Keeping at the level of our camp, we tried to enter the gorge of the Langtang Khola. Beyond the tiny fields we found ourselves in a small thicket which was succeeded by conifers, tangled with undergrowth. Here and there great boulders reared up among the trees to tower over them. The going was rough and very slow and we would have been better with an axe or a kukri to cut away the thorny stuff round our feet. Climbing one huge excrescent boulder, we found the terrain ahead continued to be rough and thorny until the shoulder swung round and out of our sight. The ground at our feet dropped sheer to the river. By leaning out we could just see it boiling in rock cauldrons below. The wall on the opposite side rose to a great height. The slopes topping it might offer a route upstream, but those on our side were more practicable and that was not saying much.

We heard a twig snap in the forest near us. At that moment Monica remarked that we might well be in bear country. We decided unanimously to return to camp and to leave the Langtang Khola until all the other valleys had had been explored.

When we returned we found the camp swarming with Sherpas—Monica declared, " We have Sherpas like other

The One Way to the Glaciers

people have mice "—and we were deafened by their excited comment and the shrill, unbroken voices of the young porters. They were eager to see all we did and ate, and were quite uninhibited—we decided there was no such thing as a shy Sherpa. It is quite probable that they had never seen a white woman before, certainly not in their own valleys complete with tents, air-mattresses and binoculars.

We decided it was best to let them satisfy their curiosity, once and for all. They were enthusiastic about the map, one planting his chin on Monica's shoulder to see better. When we pointed out their own mountains and valleys to them, they seemed to grasp the idea of how they were represented, and found them again for others. Compass, scissors, torches, all had to be examined and if possible taken apart, our knives being whisked from their sheaths before we could clap a hand on them. Yet in all the time they were with us we lost only one groundsheet, and that was left behind on a bush.

In the late afternoon an old woman from the huts nearby brought us a present of hot potatoes, baked in their jackets. She laughed hoarsely when we pantomimed for her benefit, competing for the biggest potatoes and exclaiming over their flavour. Our pleasure was real, for our menus had palled already and we were glad of anything to relieve the monotony.

We decided to have a fire of our own that night, because it was now much cooler than before, when the sun went down, and we did not see why everyone should have social evenings but ourselves. We had only to lift a branch or two for our intention to be realised, and immediately Sherpas and porters began to hack down dead trees. Admittedly, the porters' enthusiasm sprang from their eagerness to try our wood-axe, which had struck them as a pretty slipshod, useless piece of work. After making a fool of it

89

for a bit, they resorted to their kukris, which for all but the thickest branches were more efficient.

Our camp-fire was a mistake, for it allowed the Tempa-thang Sherpas to watch us in greater comfort and we had no peace. At one time they were all round us, warming their backs at the fire which we could not see ourselves. Tensing Lama was in great form and, if we addressed a remark to one another, he would pretend to take it up and join the conversation or would invent a Sherpa pun upon something we had said. This was so hilariously received that he repeated all his best jokes several times. On the march back to Kathmandu, when he had become used to us himself, Tensing Lama was the most officious in sending others about their business.

At supper-time we told them we preferred to eat in private and, in response to this and a shove or two from Mingma, they moved off reluctantly, as if they thought it was very unsporting of us to take this line. After supper, we sang to ourselves and some of the younger boys crept back to listen.

Just before getting into my sleeping-bag, I retired among the bushes. A moment later two or three porters came past carrying a huge flaming torch of bamboo. Discreetly I took a backward step, but my foot met the empty air. At the same moment, too late, the noise of the river came up, loudly and warningly. As I fell I clutched at random. My hand closed on a branch, which swung down under my weight, but held. I scrambled up again in a moment, but in the morning I saw that I had narrowly escaped falling in the dark, hundreds of feet to the Pulmutang Khola.

We did not get off to a prompt start in the morning. Most of the porters had slept in a cave but some lay under the tarpaulin, which they pulled up to their chins like a bedspread and, after our breakfast, they were still completing their toilet underneath it. It was not until 8 a.m. that Mingma had them all moving and even then they were discovered " resting " with ill-concealed grins round the first corner, like a lot of troublesome children.

Gradually the bed of the river rose to meet the track, which climbed up and down above it like a switchback. Sometimes we were walking through long grass, sometimes through curtains of tree-moss, trailing diaphanous stuff more proper to a stage-set for " Comus," than to a real live forest.

At one halt we heard Murari struggling with the Sherpa language. He was an intelligent lad, eager to learn, but he was having as much difficulty with pronunciation as we had and his efforts were regarded as equally comic. Presently everyone joined in and, far from being unlettered as we had supposed, Ang Droma got Murari to write out our numbers for her in Nepali script. For the rest of the morning we kept step to the chant, " chik, ni, soong, shi," and the Sherpas to resounding cries of " one, two, three, four."

It seemed a suitable time to reward the porters in front with a cigarette, to demonstrate goodwill and encourage those in the rear to speed up, but the only result was that Tensing Lama kept trying to cadge cigarettes from me after that—British cigarettes were a great treat. They made their own from coarse tobacco, wrapped in a leaf, and " drank " them from a clenched fist.

At another halt Ang Droma, who liked to throw sweetie papers into the wind and see them whipped away, thought of a new game. She wrapped small stones in the papers and left them on the path to trick the others as they arrived. When anyone did fall for this, there was no end to the chaff and laughter. Sherpas are economical with jokes and one like this will last them for weeks.

In an hour or so we reached a couple of bamboo shelters,

where a small family were grazing their beasts, half yak, half cow. The porters stopped for a meal and a gossip here, and there was no getting them to leave. We felt like despairing schoolmarms with an unruly class. Evelyn made the most impression, quietly telling each one to get going, and a fellow with a wispy beard and a mouth-organ was the only one to defy her openly, trying to raise a laugh at her expense. We decided to get rid of him at the first opportunity.

About noon we reached the junction between the Pulmu-tang and a big river coming in on our left. We decided this must be the Rakhta Khola, which was to lead us to the Dorje Lakpa glacier. But Nima Lama indicated we should cross it, not follow it. We looked anxiously to see if his track went along the far bank. Immediately we saw that it did not. Just above its junction with the Pulmutang, the Rakhta Khola issued from a huge slit in bare rock. This gorge, like an alley-way between two great tenement buildings, was the gateway to our glacier. We were pretty certain that even now when the river was at its lowest, it would be impossible to force a way through that gorge.

We examined the slopes on either side carefully. On the right were huge slabs lightly whiskered with grass. On the left was a steep forbidding spur, thinly forested, the skeletal rock showing through. This spur, we felt sure, would offer a route, but not one that would be suitable for loaded men. We discovered later that a few of the local people had found a way up there with their goats. Meantime, however, anyone who knew of the existence of this route was careful not to mention it for fear of giving us ideas.

Even now the river was difficult to cross, and we had to build a bridge. We found three young pines which had been used to make an earlier bridge, then carefully laid aside, and we reassembled these over the fierce, central part of the torrent, wedging them roughly together with stones. The Sherpas were very light-hearted about crossing by it, though the pines had a tendency to roll a bit under the feet.

It was 1.30 p.m. before Evelyn arrived with the last of the porters. They announced that we would have to stop here as there was no other camp-site now for a very long way. We thought this statement suspect, but could not argue. As far as we could see there was no site on the bank of the Rakhta Khola either, and if it had been our idea to camp there we were pretty sure they would have raised an outcry. As it was, they widened some small clearings in the wood above the river and in an amazingly short time had made room enough for the tents. These clearings were all adjoining with communicating steps and corridors through the trees. The camp was like a badly designed, warren-like house, with the cosy, lived-in atmosphere of such houses. The porters found that by rubbing a green stick on the water-carrying can they could produce three strange notes, and they spent the afternoon improvising on this instrument.

Monica and Evelyn went upstream to make sure that there was not, after all, some practicable route following the Rakhta Khola, while I had a bath in a little canvas wash-basin, wetting everything inside the tent very thoroughly except myself. They slithered on banks of steep gravel and hopped from boulder to boulder, the water slapping at their heels. Just below the slit of the gorge the river narrowed and the volume of water, concentrated in powerful streams, poured between huge, widely spaced rocks. During the monsoon this must be a terrible place. The gates of the gorge reminded them now of the wandering rocks of the *Iliad*, poised ready to slam shut on anyone venturing between them. They were quite glad they could go no farther.

They took a higher line on the way back, but discovered

nothing more, except that Monica's new boots, specially made for her, were too wide at the heel. This might have been a serious matter if we had had to do much rock-climbing, because she could not have placed her feet accurately on delicate holds in these boots. The handicap was not so noticeable on snow and ice.

We had begun to suffer from shortness of breath and this, combined with the abundance of tree-moss, made us think we must now be at about 11,000 feet. We brought out our altimeters, both of them borrowed, to check this estimate. For various reasons we had not had the chance to examine them before leaving the United Kingdom. We now found that neither registered heights above 8,000 feet. Even adding their totals together, we were not equipped to measure the Himalaya.

Knowing we were cross over the shortness of this day's march, Mingma proposed an early start for the next morning. We set out at 6 a.m. and had not gone far when we came to a big cave, which according to local tradition once sheltered a thousand lamas during an invasion from Tibet. The invaders must have come over a pass at the head of the Nosem Khola or still farther south, driving the local tribes into their mountain valleys. But for the moment we toyed with the idea that they might have come by a pass in the Jugal horseshoe itself, which we were about to re-discover. The porters lit a fire in the cave, burning bamboo canes, to show us the unexpected exits used by the smoke.

Our path now took us through woods carpeted with rotting leaves and bright primulae. We were too early for the best of the flowers and there were still patches of snow lying about, like litter left behind after a picnic. Beyond the woods was a large open meadow with a clear stream running through, not of glacier origin. This meadow, known as Pemsal, would have been a perfect camp-site for the previous night, and we were annoyed that we had not been told about it. The Tempathang men did not look on this as deception at all, but merely as a way of humouring impatient foreigners, who could not see that it all came to the same thing in the end.

They now said that the clear stream was the only good water for miles—the sediment in glacier water acts as a harmful irritant—and they proposed to have breakfast here. The next part of our route was very steep, they said, and they must fortify themselves accordingly. We had heard this story before and had found it to have no more substance than a slight increase in the gradient. We felt that the early start had been a farce and sat looking gloomily at Phurbi Chyachu, which now, against our will, we were approaching. She towered above us presenting a steep glacier, difficult on a grander scale than any we had met before. This was not the main Phurbi Chyachu glacier, the Phurbi Chyachumbu, which was still out of sight, but we were quite sure that it was the Phurbi Chyachumbu we were approaching and that it would be as steep and difficult as this lesser one.

Our Sherpas found another vegetable, a kind of cress this time, which, cooked with butter, had a pleasant nutty flavour, and we helped Ang Droma to gather some in her apron.

Our path now swung suddenly northwards, going straight uphill. For once the porters had predicted truly. We climbed for about 3,000 feet and not once during that time did the steepness relent. We gasped noisily for breath, we leant on our axes. But to the porters it was little trouble. They stepped up coolly with their loads, watching our trials with covert amusement. There were no cries from us now, urging them forward. It was all we could do to keep up.

We now had a full-length view of Phurbi Chyachu from her massive blunt head to the hem of her ice-draperies, trailing in dirty, shifting moraines. We asked the porters what its name meant, expecting some high-sounding reply. " Oh! It means the mountain looks rather like a chicken," they said vaguely.

At last the gradient eased and the porters saw fit to take a rest. We flopped down beside a tall rock, known in Sherpa as the Elephant's Head. It was so little like an elephant's head or indeed any part of an elephant, that we wondered if the local people exercised the same licence in naming their mountains and landmarks, as innkeepers over their inns.

" That gave you a lot of trouble, didn't it? " said one of the porters, grinning. There was no doubt that this climb would have been too much for a loaded party at the end of the previous day's march.

The place Nima Lama suggested for our base camp was now very near, he said. We reached it shortly after—a broad shelf, at about 14,500 feet, forming the floor of a corrie, and named Pomba Serebu. It was free of the snow which Nima Lama had led us to expect. Above was a wall of rock needles, broken up by widely fanning snow gullies, which separated us now from the main Dorje Lakpa glacier. The corrie floor dipped beyond the rim where we stood, and on this rim was a small lochan, surrounded by roofless stone shelters. These, covered in with bamboo mats, are used by the Tempathang herdsmen when they come up with their yaks before the monsoon. How they get the animals across the Rakhta Khola and up to this place we could not imagine, but once they are up they have to stay up, till the monsoon is over and the streams have subsided.

These shelters reminded us of ruined Highland crofts, and about them was the uncanny atmosphere of the lonely places of the North and West of Scotland. We preferred to go down into the dip, where we found a flat meadow among stalwart boulders. A clear stream from the lochan ran through it, and an isolated stone shelter stood to one side—an ideal "howff" for our porters. There were juniper bushes and other dwarf conifers in plenty for firewood. Except that it might be a dead end, Pomba Serebu seemed an ideal spot for a base camp.

We wanted to pay off the Tempathang men next day if possible, and must lose no time therefore in discovering whether we were in a good strategic position or not.

After lunch we split up to make two reconnaissances. Monica and I set out to climb the most straightforward of the steep snow gullies in the rock wall above camp, in the hope of finding a way over this wall or at least seeing what possibilities lay on the other side. Evelyn and Mingma crossed the grass spur bounding the corrie on the east, to look up the main Phurbi Chyachu glacier and find out if there was a practicable route on to the ice and up the glacier. If these reconnaissances failed, there would be nothing for it but to go back and try to force a way up one of the gorges we had passed below.

Monica and I had little success. The snow in the gully was soft and gluey, its surface weathered in a curious way, to seem honeycombed. Two avalanche chutes ran down it, one on either side. We kept looking down and thinking that at the worst an avalanche could only throw us on the scree. On the other hand, it is never very pleasant to be scraped on scree and we might sustain injuries enough to keep us in camp for the rest of the expedition.

About half-way up the gully, we rested by an island of rock. It began to snow and long fingers of mist plucked at the summit ridge. We could now see into a leftward-running branch of the gully, which terminated in a band of steep, vegetatious rock, which was probably loose into the bargain. It seemed to us the main gully offered a better route but there was no point in taking any further risk, for it was now certain we would see nothing from the top. The mist closed in, and what was left of the view seemed highly unattractive. We slid down again, one foot or another constantly getting stuck and tipping us forward and down the slope. It was not an encouraging introduction to Himalayan snow.

Evelyn's enthusiasm over her news brought her up to meet us. " We're really on to something," she said. She and Mingma had found themselves looking down on the Phurbi Chyachumbu glacier, which descended in a huge, frozen cascade to the Pulmutang valley. She had seen a way down to the moraine, reaching it at a point more than half-way up this ice-fall, which she thought we might be able to by-pass by a big open *bergschrund* forming a corridor on the left. She had caught glimpses through the mist of a smooth, almost level stretch of glacier above, a highway, she confidently predicted, to the heart of the Jugal Himal, and the frontier of Tibet. It was more than we had dared to hope.

When we returned from these sorties, our Sherpas came out to salaam, smiling and obviously pleased that we were now completely reinstated as mountaineers in the eyes of the Tempathang Sherpas.

All the Sherpas, climbers and porters, made merry in the " howff " that night, and it was a long time before the last of them fell asleep in mid-sentence. It occurred to us that the local people were very light-hearted over our plans to explore their mountains. They did not seem to regard the summits as sacrosanct or to care whether we reached them or not, so long as we provided a new interest, and our Sherpas, a good excuse for a party.

CHAPTER SEVEN

Discovery—New Mountains at 20,000 Feet

W<small>E NOW</small> had a day of rest but, as usually happens, it was busier than many of our climbing days.

We paid off the Tempathang men, all but two, Nima Lama and a lively youth, Lakpa. These two stayed to help carry loads to the edge of the glacier, and to fetch up some of their fellows when we were ready to return to Kathmandu. Mingma had difficulty in persuading any of them to stay, and eventually, without consulting us, offered full pay for the time spent at base. We made a fuss about this, though we honoured his promises. We were always out to correct the misapprehension which is so common nowadays, that expeditions have money to burn. The Sherpas, for instance, were strictly honest but this did not prevent them from trying to get the last anna out of us by any means they considered legitimate. The general impression seemed to be that we would never miss it.

Before they left, Monica persuaded the Tempathang men into a group to be photographed. They lost all their liveliness and posed as stiff and formal as a Victorian family group. Couldn't they laugh, she asked? The question struck them as so delightfully absurd they burst into loud and hearty guffaws, rolling on the ground, and it was a long time before they could be persuaded to stop.

Evelyn and I then had to look out enough high-altitude rations to last ourselves and the Sherpas for a five- or six-day reconnaissance of the Phurbi Chyachumbu glacier. My method was to amass everything round my feet until there seemed to be plenty of it. Evelyn's was to sort different foods into different piles, sardines here, sugar there, and then to complain we did not have enough of the things she liked. She would even sneak off with my food lists and, spotting some delicacy in a box to be opened in three or four weeks' time, would nag at me for an advance of nuts, say, or boiled ham.

We tested again all the mountain apparatus, lighting the high-altitude Primus stoves in the open air and setting up the mountain tents. One of these in particular, which had been lent to us, was very heavy. Its poles had to be fitted through slots on the outside of the thick canvas, and could never be persuaded to do this and remain jointed at the same time which would, we reflected, be trying at the height of a snow-storm. Mingma took a violent dislike to this tent and asked if he could take up the Palomine for the Sherpas instead. The Palomine was not built to withstand high wind, but it had a fly-sheet, so we decided to give it a trial.

We were already using two sleeping-bags at night. Our usual week-end one, lined with a sheet for warmth, went inside a special arctic bag with a down hood, tactlessly advertised as the " coffin " type.

We brought out our string vests, which create an air-space between the skin and woollen undergarments, allowing sweat to evaporate and so preventing the body from becoming too hot or too cold. Monica was very taken with hers, declaring that she would never be without one next her skin again. We gave Mingma a watch and he took care to

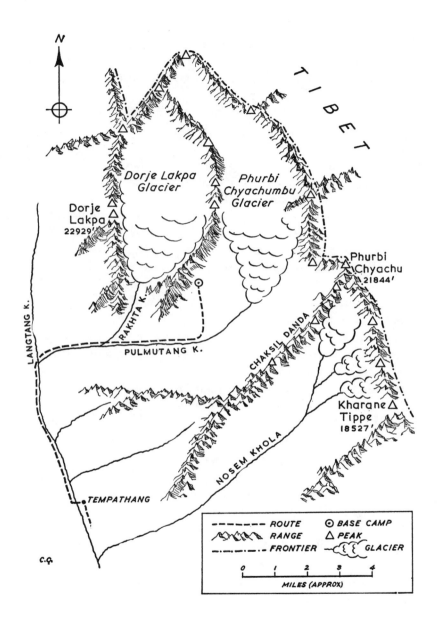

N

T I B E T

Dorje Lakpa
Glacier

Phurbi
Chyachumbu
Glacier

Dorje
Lakpa
22929'

Phurbi
Chyachu
21844'

RAKHTA K.

PULMUTANG K.

LANGTANG K.

CHAKSIL DANDA

Kharane
Tippe
18527'

NOSEM KHOLA

TEMPATHANG

C.G.

———— ROUTE   ⊙ BASE CAMP
⌃⌃⌃⌃ RANGE   △ PEAK
—·—·— FRONTIER   ⌒⌒⌒ GLACIER

0   1   2   3   4

MILES (APPROX)

show the others that he was familiar with its workings. He could tell the time very well by the sun, but the possession of a watch had the desired effect of getting him to rouse the other Sherpas on the glacier betimes.

Next morning, 24th April, we reached the crest of the grassy spur, which Evelyn had rounded with Mingma. The moraine of the Phurbi Chyachumbu glacier was far below, a mass of snow-upholstered boulders bordering gritty ice, on neither of which it seemed likely we should find a comfortable couch. Nor did it seem half so easy to reach this unattractive spot as Evelyn had talked us into imagining. On the descent we should have to move left-ward and cross two deep gullies, snow-filled, but banked on either side with mud and scree, like slag heaps in consistency. In the first of these the snow was ominously lined with brown—the tracks of falling stones. Half-way across, a small avalanche had bared a slope of frozen mud, some boulders stuck in it as impermanently as raisins in a dump-ling. On these we crossed, kicking away the looser stuff. Ang Droma had difficulty with a carelessly-bound load of firewood, which she had collected on the way. She would only cross when Evelyn, moving backwards, held her hand, but Murari was very quick and sure-footed, supported only by my black umbrella.

It surprised us, therefore, when he announced he was going back, the more so since he had been eager to accom-pany us that morning. We told him to stay where he was till Ang Droma and the porters returned.

The snow came on at this point, much earlier than the day before. We did not realise it yet, but a monsoon current was setting in, bringing with it a routine of afternoon cloud and snow. During the march we had been able to see the peaks clearly all day. Now if we were lucky the clouds held off till 1 p.m., but more often they were up by noon and on the whole, they came earlier each day as time went on. Often this hindered our exploration.

Left behind, Murari became cold and, being city-bred, could not stand the loneliness of the mist for long. Eventually he came as far as the moraine camp, but cared so little for the raw cold and the ugliness of the séracs that he never asked to come again. This was convenient, yet made us sad. He had a sensitive, venturesome spirit and a certain nimbleness, the makings of a good mountaineer, and we did not like to see them going to waste.

The porters had come over the snow bare-foot and with bare hands. Nima Lama pulled down the long woollen sleeves of his shirt, but Lakpa, who combined charm with a remarkable sense of theatre, had succeeded in getting Evelyn to lend him a pair of gloves. She now asked him to give them back. An incredulous look came into his eyes, which shortly after appeared to brim with tears. He blew pathetically on those fingers which had begun to protrude from the gloves, and she had not the heart to insist, remembering a second spare pair in her sack. Apparently there was no such word as " lend " in Sherpa.

We sent these two and Bahu off with some cigarettes as baksheesh, received in cupped hands, and Murari begged one too, fortifying himself to accompany them with Ang Droma.

We then turned to examine our new quarters. A glacier moraine is never remarkable for its beauty of landscape. This one reminded me of a station lavatory. The ice was like unwashed tiling, the rumblings of stone-fall and avalanche like trains coming and going purposelessly. The séracs and ice-blocks above assumed obscene and mocking shapes. We were on a small rise, protected from toppling séracs on the one hand and from stone-fall on the other, and as this was our first true Himalayan camp, which no one had promised us would be romantic or even comfortable, we settled down without complaint.

On the whole our high camps were more comfortable than many I have endured in the arctic conditions of a Scottish winter, when I was much less well-equipped and no one cooked my dinner.

We had two small mountain tents for ourselves, and slept two memsahibs in one, and one in the other. We kept changing round to keep our relationships in smooth running order. Sometimes I found it a relief to have a tent to myself and to arrange it to my own satisfaction (not necessarily neatly), and to be able to put on my underpants or blow my nose without feeling I was inconveniencing someone else. (The others said I blew my nose like a trumpet, and that they could tell the time by it for reveille or lights out. This is a gross exaggeration.) At other times I wanted to know what the others were laughing and talking about.

At meal-times we foregathered, usually in the tent for two, which was then reduced to a state of mild chaos, kettles precariously perched on rucksacks and jam emptying itself quietly into a sleeping-bag. The task of spreading biscuits and concocting drinks fell to the one slow enough to be left nearest the door.

Next morning the snow was still falling in a stealthy, persistent way, laying a cloak over the tents, our tracks and the crevasses, as if with the sinister purpose of reducing everything to a featureless white expanse. I was actively sick and could hardly lift my head, which felt as though a painful weight were clamped to it. It was difficult to account for this, since we could hardly be much higher than at base camp where I had felt no ill-effects from oxygen-lack. Strangely enough, this was the only time I ever suffered from mountain sickness. Acclimatisation seemed to me like going through a sound barrier. Once this altitude, critical for me, was past, I had not much trouble, except poor appetite and, of course, breathlessness. Monica expressed it as " acclimatising with a click," in her case, on the stiff pull-up to base camp.

One thing I learned with relief—that mountain sickness is not a purely psychological reaction or the result of a mental set. Monica had spoken of it scornfully to bolster me up.

" You can nearly always overcome mountain sickness if you are determined enough, I think," she said. " Most people wouldn't have half so much trouble if they had never heard of it. Best thing you can do is to pretend it doesn't exist." I became more apprehensive than ever on hearing this, feeling sure that I would suffer in such an acute and prolonged form as to demonstrate clearly my lack of will-power and proneness to suggestion. Yet the sickness passed off quickly and I was never again unable to eat.

Evelyn, on the other hand, had sensibly given the matter no thought. Yet she suffered more than myself, and sometimes continuously for several days, though she might have gone higher with comfort, if we had spent a longer time in the mountains.

We decided not to move on that day into bad weather and unknown territory, but in the afternoon it cleared slightly. Since Monica was the fittest, for Evelyn felt a little seedy, too, at this height, she set off with Mingma and Ang Temba to reconnoitre a route through that part of the ice-fall above camp. We watched anxiously as they made their way up through the narrowing corridor of the *bergschrund*, which by-passed the maze of séracs and pinnacles in midstream and led to the upper part of the glacier. This corridor was constantly under the threat of falling stones, which made it highly unsafe, and we had already rejected it as a through route. In the afternoon it sounded as if a pitched battle was going on, some of the stones falling quite near camp and hurling themselves savagely on everything in their path as if angry at being displaced. Evelyn and I were relieved to see the others find a way out, up on to the ice itself. We caught sight of them only occasionally after that, creeping over huge snow-covered blocks or perched on spires of ice.

To Monica the reconnaissance must have been like a topographical game of snakes and ladders, played out in sober earnest. Now they would make a mistaken trail, leading to an impasse, where a huge black pocket of ice waited as the penalty for a false move. Now they would find the right line and be rewarded by a shining upward-leading crest into the next puzzle. Mingma cut steps with dash and vigour—he was always at his best in a situation of this kind—and Monica followed, cutting intermediate steps, the result exactly fitting her stride. But in spite of the séracs raised in threat above, and the crevasses lurking below, Mingma was reluctant to put on the rope.

This reluctance to rope was the only difficulty we had with our Sherpas. They went where we wanted to go, respecting our judgment, and though Mingma made excellent suggestions as to the route, he left the final decision to us. Mingma and Ang Temba showed more initiative in climbing than the others, Mingma, who is a competent and experienced mountaineer, being especially keen to lead. We did not discourage them because it was better to share the work of trail-breaking and step-cutting with the Sherpas, whose strength, obviously, was greater than ours. They identified themselves more closely with our project as a result. They did not think it odd that women should be tackling this kind of thing, for their own women, though they do not climb on snow and ice, are tough and adventurous.

Sherpas are not dominated by their own women, however, and tactless management of them on our part would have been disastrous.

We were glad that Mingma and Ang Temba had something of the true spirit of mountaineering and a love of adventure, even though these were allied to a blithe disregard for objective danger (except stone-fall which they treated with great respect). So far few Sherpas have wanted to climb mountains for their own sake, and none have planned an expedition on their own account. Tenzing, of course, is a notable exception and others will follow him. Eventually the Sherpas may become guides and leaders, in the same way as Swiss guides, climbing better than amateurs, evolved from the Swiss porter-peasant of the mid-nineteenth century. As yet Sherpas know little of map and compass work or of mountain rescue, but already a school of mountaineering has been opened for them in Darjeeling.

The rope was put on, and Mingma perfunctorily showed Ang Temba how to belay. Ang Temba drove his axe into an inch or two of snow, which would never have held in case of a fall. Such behaviour made the rope more of a danger than a safeguard and several times Monica had to insist on a better belay.

" *Thik hai*, memsahib," Ang Temba would say lightheartedly, meaning that everything was fine. The only cure for him, we thought, was to fall right into a crevasse —but we had no wish for it to be administered in the course of our expedition.

They reached the almost level stretch of the glacier above before returning. Monica came back to the tent and overwhelmed us with enthusiasm and snow.

" Look, there's a simply splendid route through the ice-fall," she said. " We'll be able to go right up this glacier." Mingma hovered outside to have some part in bringing the good news, and all we could see of him was a huge grin, like the Cheshire cat's.

The following morning was clear and fine and I felt well again. I was so glad that I got up before 5 a.m. The others considered my *joie de vivre* ill-timed, and the Sherpas, who had been such prompt risers on the march, were not so easily got out of their survival suits on a glacier. The morning was bitterly cold and we seemed to be in the niche last reached by the sun. The snow was blue and iron-hard, barely taking a foot-print, and my fingers became numb in a moment. Eventually Monica and Evelyn got up and sat on an air-bed in all the clothes they possessed, frozen in reproachful attitudes, and waited for the sun to reach us. At last it touched our immobilised camp and, like the kiss that woke the Sleeping Beauty, brought life and sparkle to the snow, to the Sherpas, and to ourselves.

I do not mean to convey that there was anything beautiful about our appearance at the time. We did wash at this camp, but we gave up the practice immediately, since all our water had to be got by melting snow. We were in a clean world and it was too cold anyhow. Our hair became straight and lank, though we combed it now and again, and I kept mine out of sight under a yellow cap or the balaclava which alternated with it as a wig. Monica's became bleached and very dry for it had been given too strong a " perm " before leaving home and it was beginning to fall out. She had to break one of our capsules of castor-oil over it, rubbing the contents in.

In spite of certain popular assertions in the Indian press, we did not wear make-up or lipstick on our climbs, let alone at 22,000 feet. This would have been highly dangerous. Even under a thick protective coating of glacier cream, which looked like the theatrical make-up for an unpleasant character-part, we were burnt by the fierce ultra-violet rays of the sun at these heights, reinforced by their reflection from the snow. My lips, constantly parted in the struggle for breath, were severely burnt inside where the cream had got licked off. Drinking orange juice became an exquisite torture to me.

Each time we moved camp we had to move everything with us, like tinkers. Sometimes we made a cache for food but we could not afford the tents to leave supporting camps. It often took a long time to pack up in the cold, though the Sherpas became more practised as time went on. Usually we had to wait until the sun reached the tents, melting the scintillating ice-sheaths, and the frozen skirtings which kept them firmly stuck to the snow.

It was well after 8 o'clock on the first morning when we entered the huge maze of the ice-fall. Mingma started ahead of the others with his load and was half-way up the first pitch, clearing the steps of new snow, before we could reach him. We had no choice then but to rope, in cramped positions, with Mingma at the head of the first rope and Evelyn leading the second. I went next to Mingma, as I was more likely to hold him if he fell than Monica, who is small and light. I found it slightly unnerving for, embarrassed by his top-heavy load, he made the same panicky little noises at a crucial move as when he gambled. Each time, fortunately, this was followed by the little squeal of triumph which greeted the dice well thrown.

At one place we had to cross a slender bridge of ice. At another we climbed an ice-wall terminating in a sharp knife-edge, and leapt across an unexpected crevasse beyond. We were too pre-occupied to realise that the clouds were coming up, until we found ourselves engulfed.

When we came out on the flat of the glacier above, still harassed by the criss-cross of crevasses, we could see the knobs of a long snow-covered central moraine leading up into the mist—the glacier's vertebrae. We took a compass bearing on this before the mist settled—15°—and marched on it for over an hour. But first, having reached easier ground, we could stop and change places on the rope. Monica took over the lead from Mingma, for we wanted to do our own route-finding. In any case, as she pointed out to him, if she fell into an unsuspected crevasse, she was easily hauled out again. She would be like a pea on a string compared with the bulk of Mingma and his load. Shortly afterwards this was proved when she did slip into a hidden crevasse—to waist level only. She said it was like crashing through a skylight window, the ice tinkling like glass far below.

The clouds parted only slightly and occasionally. The glacier seemed to narrow, and a new ice-fall appeared coming in on the left. We decided to camp while still sure we were out of danger from avalanche. We found a flat stretch and Mingma and Ang Temba shuffled up and down, trampling down the snow to make a place for the tents. This was a regular performance known as the " tent dance." Meanwhile we tramped out a path of our own across two crevasses to the far side of the spinal moraine, where we succeeded in finding cover.

The Sherpas always observed which boulder or hollow we adopted and quietly selected another, usually less accessible. If they met one of us returning from the Ladies' they would pretend not to see us at all, and if it were first thing in the morning, would reserve their greeting for the next encounter.

This afternoon followed the pattern of many others. We sat in the tents listening to the sharp crepitation or soft caress of the falling snow which consolidated, then cracked into slates and slid off, a sleeping-bag wrapped round our feet or our shoulders. Ang Temba would bring us leafy tea or an Ovaltine brew called " Ovocha ", which was more acceptable at these heights, and sardines and Macvita. Often he was singing a little song which he had just made up to commemorate some incident in camp. There is one, composed on the occasion of his learning the word for raisin, which runs thus :

> *Gudrun, raisin,*
> *Gudrun, raisin; gudrun,*
> *Raisin; gudrun, raisin.*

He brought us our evening meal also and if the Sherpas had thought up some special treat, like salmon, Kusung would come too and poking his head round the door, would shout, " Salaam, memsahib," with a grin, as if to indicate the whole thing had been his idea, and then sit back to watch the effect.

We read or wrote till evening, preferring books with some real matter to them. We had been advised that we should want to exercise our minds and this was true, though Evelyn found that to study her *Applied Physiology* was carrying things too far. I myself best enjoyed *Grey Eminence*, whose meaning I could not catch by light skimming. Monica spent a great deal of time with the *Confessions of Rousseau*, though latterly his defections became a little tedious, and *The Brothers Karamazov* was popular, until it was found that I had forgotten to bring Part II on the expedition. Much of Monica's time was spent in planning a new wardrobe, and of Evelyn's and mine in conjuring up hearty if not *soigné* meals. I sometimes felt a great longing to hear good music, though I do not often listen to music at home.

After our evening meal we got into both sleeping-bags with our wet socks and gloves, which we put between the two layers of down to dry out. Our boots had to come in, too, and they lay on the feet all night like a cold chupatti on the stomach. Even so, they were often frozen hard in the morning.

My only real discomfort at night was that I could not sleep with my head right inside my bag as I do at home. If I tried to do this I woke struggling desperately for air and my face came in contact with the searing cold of the zip-fastener. It was bad enough with my head out, for I found myself gasping as if after great exertion when I turned over, or even when I thought of it and then changed my mind.

Next morning the walls of the tent were bellied inward with the weight of newly fallen snow. A thump or two from inside cleared this away, and the sun shone through. I struggled out, half-asleep, having no idea of what I should see. The impact of the scene and the cold air outside woke me at once into startled awareness. A peak stood at the head of the glacier which I had not seen before, shapely and beautifully buttressed, glowing with great intensity in the rich yellow light of the early sun. It seemed to leap from a sky of darkest blue. I felt as though a sudden splendid chord of music had rung out across the sky and I wanted to shout aloud. I did shout, for the others looked out, muttering grouses which were immediately silenced.

Each morning had the same quality of excitement about it in our high camps; a quality which did not necessarily hale us out of our sleeping-bags, but—this was its special attraction—which could be savoured in anticipation and in comfort. We never could tell what we would find on looking out; what new unclimbed, unnamed mountains would have taken shape in the mists of the previous day's advance, or what new and perhaps terrible aspects of the mountains we had already seen would have appeared to shock and humble us. If I had ever entertained any ideas of " proving myself " against these mountains, I lost them now for good.

The sun reached us earlier this morning and the snow,

spread everywhere unwrinkled, was beaded and sparkling. We got off to a good start, though Evelyn was suddenly sick in the snow. The Sherpas murmured sympathetically and with unfailing courtesy averted their eyes and made no fuss. The worst of this sickness was that it made her feel no better afterwards. She kept going, however, slowly and with valiant effort, stopping often to clean her goggles which had steamed, and often cleaning her goggles in order to stop.

Though I felt sympathy for her, I could not conceal my excitement. We were crossing a narrow neck at the head of the lower part of the glacier, which then opened out into a huge white horse-shoe, surrounded by magnificent peaks and their attendant glaciers, each poised over the central one in a lingering fall. No one had ever been here or seen all this before.

It is impossible for most human beings to sustain for long such feelings as we now experienced and much of our time and attention in this splendid horse-shoe, unrivalled by anything in our imagination, was taken up with mundane, trivial things. Yet the thought of these trivial things—the way Ang Temba carried his axe upside down, for instance, making patterns in the snow for fun, recalls in a moment the whole splendour of our situation, and all the wonder and joy we felt in it.

When we were well up in this new basin, we decided to camp. The mist was already closing in, blotting out the magnificent cirque and surrounding us instead with grey, indefinable walls. We had seen, however, that the rim of our basin, which to the north and east formed the frontier ridge between Nepal and Tibet, dipped low between Phurbi Chyachu and the shapely peak we had discovered at the head of our glacier. We might reach this dip by a long steep spur just above camp and from it see Tibet. We wanted, too, to have a closer look at the north ridge of

Phurbi Chyachu, whose crest rose steeply but then levelled out. This crest is no more substantial in places than a leaf of ice, yet we were deceived by its angle into thinking we might find a route along it. At the same time we wanted to examine the shapely peak to the north of the dip, which had quite captivated us. We had begun to call it " Ladies' Peak," with a previousness shortly to be reprimanded. Its western skyline was steep in the lower part but to our inexperienced eyes suggested a broad buttress which might be climbed.

Evelyn sank down on a plump kitbag as soon as we stopped, and Ang Temba and Chhepela had her installed in her tent so quickly, it seemed as if they had pitched it round her. Chhepela had been quick to master our system of changing places in the tents and never failed to arrange our kitbags and sleeping-bags accordingly. But Kusung could not get hold of the idea and always looked dismayed as if he were saying, " Surely they haven't gone and changed again? "

In the morning another surprise was sprung upon us. We emerged to find twin peaks to the west of us, the sun rolling down their flanks of rock and ice in a warm, brilliant tide. One was slightly higher than the other, and the two looked rather like the mountain we had identified from a distance as Dorje Lakpa. It was only a short step from this to decide that this *was* Dorje Lakpa and, since we felt at liberty to discredit the map entirely, we developed a pretty theory that there were not two main glaciers in the Jugal, but one. " In any case," we argued in our innocence, " the whole of the Jugal Himal could not contain two glaciers as big as the one we are now exploring." The ridge above our base camp separated us only from the small glaciers of the western valley, we said, and all the main peaks of the Jugal horseshoe were ranged above us now in a single magnificent sweep.

Discovery—New Mountains at 20,000 Feet

Evelyn felt better this morning and decided to climb with us to the dip in the rim of peaks between " Ladies' Peak " and Phurbi Chyachu. The steep slope to the east leading up to the dip wore a silky blue sheen, indicating ice below a skin of snow. The slope was not crevassed till very near the top but might readily become a colossal and expeditious chute. I studied it for a moment, then reached for my crampons.

It was my turn to lead one rope and Mingma led the other, shooting ahead now that he had no load and pulling Evelyn after him at such a pace she had to call a halt every fifty yards or so. If she had gone at her own pace, she would have been able to keep going. I was not averse to halting myself, each time I got myself and my party up in line with the others, but Monica was very fit and going well, with great drive. She and Mingma should have cast themselves off from the rest of us and hurried on, for already the clouds were gaining on us. But we did not think of this in time.

Monica's fitness was not only due to the fact that she had already climbed to 21,000 feet in Sikkim and acclimatised more easily a second time. At lower altitudes she is a fast walker both on the flat and going uphill. In her childhood and early youth she spent much of her time in the jungles of South India, keeping up with a striding, absent-minded father on the trail of big game. Monica is only 5 feet 1 inch in height. There is no ideal shape or size for a man when it comes to Himalayan climbing—as witnessed by the diversity of the Everest and Kanchenjunga teams. But it may well be that the small woman scores at great heights, if she is wiry and spirited. Claude Kogan, who has been higher than any other woman in the world, stands barely 5 feet in her socks. It is my guess the first woman to stand on the summit of Mount Everest will be small-boned and petite.

For some way the snow-skin adhered to the ice below and we could kick steps in it. We were climbing the left wall of a long, white spur, which steepened as we neared the crest. The ice bared itself, glistening and treacherous. With one accord we stopped to put on crampons—all except Ang Temba who indicated that he had found his too big. His only regret at not having brought them was, no doubt, that it would have been a good laugh to see himself shuffling about in them now.

I discovered that the supposedly foolproof fastenings of my crampons which had seemed so easy and elegant in Kathmandu, were now jammed at the hinges with ice. Ang Temba wound himself round one boot, Chhepela round the other, but to no avail. The things would not shut. Kusung offered me a bit of string, delighted to have had an idea at last, but after a step or two this broke. I decided to cut steps, which were necessary for Ang Temba anyhow. Neither the dusting of snow nor the adamant ice would hold a well-driven axe to act as a belay for him.

I went over the crest, feeling as if I were chipping my way up a huge upturned pudding-bowl, and Ang Temba lolloped after.

This led to a little hollow in the crest of the spur, about 500 feet below the frontier ridge. It was filling in rapidly with dank mist and we knew there was no hope of this clearing. We would see nothing from the top. There was no point in going farther.

Consoling ourselves with the thought that this climb was good for acclimatisation—we probably reached 18,500 feet, since we felt certain at the time that it was 20,000 feet—we turned downhill. When we reached my ice-steps on the way down, I told Kusung and Ang Temba to move with care, trying to get them to understand that I could not belay them properly. But they skidded about quite unconcerned, chopping bigger steps with the idea of pleasing me, though ill-balanced on those already cut.

This moment seems hair-raising to me in retrospect yet at the time I do not think I was more than annoyed. Altitude seemed to make us less anxious, even a little less responsible than if we had been climbing on lower ranges.

The mountains we saw were at times no less terrible than I had imagined and we did move among them chastened and with circumspection. The first sight of an appalling crevasse, like the door of the underworld opening at Persephone's feet, would leave an indelible impression and be remembered afterwards with awe. Yet at the time we regarded them with a certain objectivity. Paradoxically, I never felt so keyed-up or apprehensive before a day's expedition, as at home or in the Alps. This was one reason why climbing in the Himalaya was quite a different experience from any I have attempted elsewhere and, in one way, more pleasurable—that is, until we reached an altitude of about 20,000 feet, when each step cost too much of an effort to be anything but pain.

It seemed, too, that we took precautions more from habit and training than from any sense of fear. For this reason, if no other, we concluded that it was important for most members of a Himalayan expedition to have previous experience of climbing on snow and ice.

This lessening of anxiety, amounting at times to serenity, together with a constant awareness of our surroundings, had an unexpected effect on our relations with one another. Contrary to expectation, these were always good in the mountains. Most climbers of Himalayan experience maintain that companions who seem the best of fellows on weekend climbs become odious to one another in high camps, each failing being thrown into relief, each mannerism becoming an intolerable irritation. W. H. Murray goes so far as to say, " I could cheerfully have slain every one of my companions at quite frequent intervals, but for the need of tiresome explanations to relatives." For this reason members of big expeditions are chosen for equability of temperament as much as for climbing skill.

Some of these Himalayan climbers maintain that altitude is not responsible for these difficulties, at least not up to a height of 20,000 feet or so, so much as living together in tents over a long period, in discomfort and boredom, and our experience certainly bore this out. We were tempted to conclude that women are better able to endure these discomforts—and to occupy themselves during the long hours which must be spent in Himalayan camps.

At any rate the only effect of altitude itself upon our relationship was that it made us more kindly affectioned to one another. Evelyn it is true, lost all her usual liveliness for a time, but she acquired a new dignity, and showed great unselfishness and concern lest she might keep us back—as she did not. Indeed she developed a really beautiful character hitherto unsuspected. It was in the plains of India, when we were subjected to heat and dust and the constant worry of saying the right things to reporters and Customs officials, and of typing lists and captions and articles on trains and in waiting-rooms, that we quarrelled. Then we had the small upsets and the bickerings which no doubt we were pictured by some people as having in the mountains.

We had thought of making a quick dash up to the frontier ridge the next day, but the opportunity had gone. It was a sullen morning and iron-grey clouds were already in possession above. We had little food left and must return to base camp that day. This we did quickly and with a will, for we were bent on returning to explore this glacier more thoroughly as soon as possible.

We travelled unroped for a time on firm snow. Two

lammergeyers, the bearded vultures of the Himalaya, went gliding overhead with hardly a flicker of the wing, studying us, we imagined, through lowered lids. At this reminder of our mortality we stopped and insisted on roping, though we were still well above the ice-fall and Mingma obviously regarded this as fussy. Not long after, he sank into two or three crevasses himself in rapid succession, though he remained buoyed up by his load, which jammed across the hole made by his body. The second time Ang Temba ran up to help him out, standing then himself on snow that was proved unsafe, instead of belaying him from a firm stance. Evelyn and I shouted to him simultaneously, but in our agitation got the wrong name.

"Kusung! Go back, Kusung!" we yelled.

And poor old Kusung turned round as much as to say, "Who, me?" while Ang Temba continued to wrestle in such a way as to precipitate both himself and Mingma into the depths at any moment.

We had some difficulty in finding the start of our route down through the ice-fall in the mist. The snow had wiped away our tracks completely, like a fussy housewife cleaning up after guests before they have had time to go. The clouds had been running before a storm, which was now gathering force. The gloom was lit up by quick flashes and the snow, falling gently, stirred to the sound of thunder. Our snow goggles became blurred, which was exasperating, especially for Monica, for hers were fitted with the lenses which she normally wears. She was not able to see with them or without them. Moreover she maintains she cannot hear without glasses either. We took this statement with a pinch of salt until we noticed that she reached for them whenever the conversation became interesting.

Mingma was so anxious to get beyond the threat of falling stones in the last short stretch through the *berg-*

schrund, that he covered it at a run, pulling Monica from her steps on the ice-pitch and causing her to wrench her knee again.

As we approached camp there was a sudden shout and a crash, announcing Bahu. Mingma had told him to come and look for us at the foot of the ice-fall every day from the fifth day after our departure. He seemed delighted to see us, no doubt because he would not have to come and meet us again, and he had brought up some yak's milk, still warm in a Thermos flask, a present from the Tempathang Sherpas. We found it had a strong flavour, suggesting a dirty dairy, which took possession of everything it was used for, cocoa, porridge or custard.

After a short rest, we set off back to base camp. The porters and Ang Droma came out to salaam and Murari rather self-consciously said, " How d'you do," but base camp was not the warm cheerful haven we had been picturing. The tents were surrounded by slush and seemed draughty, the fire was smoking and the storm was still knocking about the sky. If this kind of weather settled in, we should never get back to the frontier ridge or see anything more. In depressed silence we fell asleep.

CHAPTER EIGHT

A Vital Pass

ON THE morning after our return to base camp, the 30th of April, Mingma bustled about improving its amenities. He sent the two porters up to the deserted shelters above us for a long stout prayer flag-pole and some half-rotten bamboo roofing. The pole he placed lengthwise across the " howff " as an elementary roof-tree and over it draped the bamboo mats and our tarpaulin, to make a sanctified and fairly weatherproof store and kitchen. The outdoor kitchen had been flagged with stones in our absence, drained and provided with shelves. It was fenced to windward by a huge semi-circle of firewood, thatched with juniper, and some kindling had been put aside under an overhanging boulder to keep dry.

We so far recovered our spirits as to want a bath, and fetched out a square canvas tub. The Sherpas were quite carried away by the idea, and erected a fly-sheet as a bath shelter for our privacy, dug a hollow inside for the bath and a runnel flowing from it as waste-pipe. They set two cans, one full of hot water, one of cold, beside the bath and a bamboo carrying-basket to hold our dirty clothes.

We did not suggest any of this—they worked it out for themselves. They got a great deal of fun out of thinking up ploys to please us and remembered for future reference those which had succeeded. On this occasion they got more fun out of it than we did, for we were committed and there was nothing for it but to bathe.

For my own amusement I took photographs of my friends in the tub, showing the snowdrifts piled round the shelter and the anguished expressions on their faces. But unfortunately I forgot to extract the roll of film on which they appeared, from the package we sent to be processed in America under the auspices of a popular journal, which had taken an option on our material. My friends worked themselves up into a state of great alarm, picturing themselves on the front cover of this journal in the altogether. Wires were sent, messages were flown, in a desperate attempt to retrieve the offending roll, but in the end the tin containing all the films was discovered lying delayed and neglected in Delhi. The roll, which was then hastily extracted, was appropriately labelled STARK 19.

We repaired the ravages made to our faces by sun and snow burns, though fortunately our metal mirrors were so scratched they did not give an exact image. We did not realise just how roughened our complexions were till, at a meeting of the British Women's Association in Bombay, a stranger approached us and, introducing herself as a beauty specialist, asked concernedly if she might give us each a free facial.

Ang Droma took possession of all our clothes and washed them thoroughly, pounding the soaped garments on stones until there was not much soap left and, we imagined, very little garment. I slipped her some underwear very discreetly, but a little later found Bahu, who had been made to help, scrubbing it in a bored sort of way. The dye from one of the Sherpa's shirts spread to our string vests, which took on a splendid purple hue. We thought this rather funny, or rather I did, for my string vest had not been sent to the wash, but Kusung's dignity was hurt. He rated

A Vital Pass

Ang Droma soundly and washed the vests again, fixing the purple dye for good. " There! I've had to do the job myself," he seemed to be saying.

The Sherpas, too, washed themselves thoroughly and regularly. We had been led to believe that they considered cleanliness a very poor second to godliness, but this was far from being the case. All had soap and mirrors and would use our nail-files surreptitiously. They did not shave, since few Sherpas have more than sparse growth, but plucked hairs from their chins with large tweezers, like pliers in appearance. They did not like to be seen doing this and often turned their backs on us until the operation was complete.

They washed their clothes too, often in our cooking *dekshis*, and mended them. Kusung had a shirt from which patches had been cut so often there was no tail or sleeve left. By this means the body-work had been very creditably preserved. The Tempathang Sherpas were more jungly and considered this kind of thing pretty soft. Perhaps my nose had become too well-adjusted to the country, but I noticed only that they were redolent of wood-smoke and hillside.

Next morning I was impatient to try again to find a way over the ridge above base camp, though we no longer believed that it separated us from the big central glacier. Having decided that this did not exist, we expected to find a series of small glaciers only on the far side.

It was decided that Monica should stay behind sensibly resting her knee, which Evelyn rebandaged, and sort out enough food for our next glacier trip, while Evelyn and I reconnoitred above camp.

We traversed round the outer rim of our corrie, ignoring the gully Monica and I had tried on the day of our arrival, for we saw its snow was even less well consolidated than before. We hoped to find a way on to the crest of the ridge above camp, away to the left where it dipped low, by an easy rock-scramble or gully. We made good progress, till suddenly and unexpectedly we came to the edge of our world. A huge cliff dropped away at our feet and we were looking dizzily into a deep glen. It was a moment or two before we collected our spinning senses and realised that this was the valley of the Pulmutang by which we had arrived. We could even see as far as the tiny green patch of the *gompa*, far below us now. Our base camp was in a small hanging corrie, as neatly fashioned in the steep hillside as if it had been scooped out with a spoon. Obviously, we could traverse no farther leftward and must turn our attention to the cliffs directly above. These were disappointingly steep, forbidding, mossy and wet. Evelyn and I could have climbed them, no doubt, with difficulty, but we could see no real line of weakness which would form a justifiable route for loaded men. There was one faint possibility, however, a cleft whose inner wall was hidden from us. We must look into it before dismissing the cliff as routeless, for this cleft might be the easy gully we were looking for.

A bank of very dark clouds was piling up on the far side of the valley, increasing the impression it gave of great depth. These clouds were approaching slowly but implacably, though it was only 11 a.m. We had no time to lose. We raced up slopes of snow-crusted turf till we came to a steep boulder-field, which slowed us at once. The boulders were piled against one another, as big as old-fashioned sideboards, and between them were large deceptive puffs of snow, which we had to sound with our axes in search of solid footing, for they concealed great holes and traps. When we reached the foot of the rocks, we saw that the cleft was not a true cleft, but a mere depression walled by a steep-angled slab on the side nearest to us. This slab was so holdless that the faintest of lines only were traced on it by the few flakes of snow that had found lodgement. No sooner had we established its real character than it disappeared. The clouds had caught up with us. At first they seemed, as often happens, to be less dark and menacing once they had actually engulfed us. But they were storm clouds for all that. The wind rose and the snow blew hard in our faces, the huge flakes shaken from time to time by thunderclap. Neither of us cared much for the prospect of edging our way down and round through the big boulders, which would now be as slippery as if they had been newly soaped. We took a higher line, heading back towards camp across a chaotic mass of smaller boulders. It took us twice as long to go back.

Monica had discouraging news for us when we reached the tents. Mingma, perturbed by her preparations for a new sortie, had declared that all the new snow and all the snow about to fall, lying deep and soft, would make the going higher up very difficult and exhausting. Loaded Sherpas would sink into it to their thighs, in crevassed areas at their peril. He thought we should wait for an improvement in the weather, which he expected in four or five days' time, before returning to the Phurbi Chyachumbu glacier.

I was dismayed. Five days! It seemed an interminable time when we were so anxious to get ahead. I searched my memory of all I had read about Himalayan climbing for some clue as to what we should now decide. The truth was that Mingma had more experience of weather and snow conditions in the Himalaya than any of us. Would we run into danger or avalanche, say, if we proceeded? Would we be wasting our time, making little progress and losing heart in these poor conditions? Monica felt that Mingma was right and Evelyn was inclined to agree. I did not want to press for a decision which might turn out to be foolhardy. We must wait and see.

I sat all afternoon looking out glumly at the mist, grained with falling snow, and then hunted for a comfortable book. I thought I had found it in Moravia's *Woman of Rome*, and prepared to suspend all disbelief in its sunny passages, but reached sordid and cheerless chapters as the early evening advanced.

Some *ram chikor*, birds which the Sherpas called "Tilling" flew overhead, making their strange evocative cry, "Tilling, tilling." Like the curlew's, it belonged to desolate moor and hillside.

Eventually Murari's tent collapsed under the weight of new snow and he had to spend the night in the " howff." But he took this in good part, having lost much of his self-consciousness by this time and become one of the boys. He was not too well, poor fellow, and we noticed he had taken to cosseting himself with Horlicks, which he had recognised as the stuff they gave the patients in the Kathmandu hospitals.

We woke next morning to find all the tents half-buried and the Sherpas clearing them, shaking snow in big sugary lumps from their walls. Everything about the camp seemed colourless in the snow-glare, and we bitterly resented having to wear snow-goggles and put on protective creams, stiff in their tubes even here, when there was no adventure and no grandeur to compensate for them. Bahu was careless about this and became snowblind later in the day.

From the look of the sky we felt sure that more snow was on the way and that we could not yet risk a second visit to the Phurbi Chyachumbu glacier. But we could make another effort to find a pass over the ridge above base. We turned our attention again to the gully Monica and I had tried on the day of our arrival, and started up early in the hope of finding a foundation of firm snow under the new stuff.

When we paused to tell Mingma our plan, we realised he felt it as a rebuke to be left out and was as interested in looking over the ridge as we were ourselves. We graciously consented to have all our food and spare clothing put in his sack, and a surprised Ang Temba was detailed to carry it, Mingma going back to his porridge in the sure knowledge that he could soon catch us up on the trail we beat out.

Ang Temba took his turn at step-kicking—or when the snow was at its worst, at swimming—upwards. He was as glad to be relieved each time as we were. The snow was so far from being consolidated it looked and behaved like rice piled high. At each step we plunged in, sometimes to the crutch. As we went higher it became steeper and the surface smoother. Little balls of snow, then whorls resembling sugar buns, came rolling down, leaving dotted trails. If these had run across the snow instead of down I would have imagined each one ticketed, " Tear along the dotted line," for the snow looked just about ready to tear apart and avalanche.

Finally Monica voiced the unhappy thought of us all.

" Do you suppose this is safe? "

Of course it was not. We had by this time reached the boulder, now freshly upholstered, where Monica and I had turned back before, and could see again into the leftward-running branch of the gully. But now the horizontal ledges and holds in the rock band forming its exit, not apparent before, were clearly picked out by the snow. It would certainly " go." What was more, the whole of this branch gully lay at an easier angle and its snow was much less deep and not likely to avalanche.

Into this branch we hurriedly traversed and when we reached the rocks, roped up, though the passage proved quite easy. Ang Temba was next to Monica, who led. But instead of belaying he scrambled up on her heels and got in the way. We yelled to him to come down.

" What was that? " he said, pretending to be absorbed in the rock-work and persevering in his folly. When he was up he turned to us with an engaging smile—" You were saying? "

He often tried this one on with Mingma too.

Meanwhile Monica, above, was giving vent to gasps of wonder and shouts of triumph, her exact words lost to us like those of radio's Mrs. Glum. We yelled back, " We don't want to hear your commentary. Take in the —— rope and let's see it. for ourselves."

The first thing I noticed as my head came over the top was that there were easy snow slopes on the far side of the ridge, by which we could at some future time descend. Thus we had discovered a true pass. We saw later, on looking back from the farther side, that we had hit on the only point on the ridge where a crossing is possible. If we had persisted in following the right branch of the gully, we would have landed ourselves above nasty, snow-plastered slabs and shaky pinnacles, unsafe to descend.

I had no time to consider the implications of this, for at once three elegant white spires, piercing blue sky, caught my attention. Facing us was a beautiful, complicated and quite unexpected mountain. There was no deception about it, no pretence of accessibility. Spired, iced and flashing, its three peaks rose with supreme confidence in their own impregnability. They woke in us no desire to take up their challenge. We merely sat and looked.

But what on earth was it? We had an uneasy feeling that it must be Dorje Lakpa, and for a moment truth struggled with our desire to preserve easily-worked-out theories. It *was* Dorje Lakpa. The formidable twin peaks

128

bounding the Phurbi Chyachumbu glacier, which we had identified as Dorje Lakpa, were something else, unnamed peaks of which our map simply took no cognizance.

Immediately below us the main Dorje Lakpa glacier asserted its existence with horrid spectacle and thunder. And here another surprise awaited us, for this glacier was not at an easy angle. It was steep, difficult and dangerous, offering nothing but discouragement, and we could thank our lucky stars that we had not reached it first. It was a mass of ice-debris, piled high, of shattered séracs and powdered pinnacles. I had never before seen a glacier in such a wholesale state of disintegration. It looked like an immense pot of mashed potatoes. It was continually collapsing with a great roaring.

By trying in our imagination to telescope two glaciers into one, we had shown a complete failure to grasp the Himalayan scale, which was now being forcibly brought home to us.

We went along the ridge for a bit, for the climbing was interesting, of mixed rock and snow with entertaining pitches, and we were still at an altitude where these could be enjoyed. We saw that the third top of Dorje Lapka swung away from the other two and lay well north of them. It may count as a separate mountain, not marked on the map. It is just possible, too, that it may prove accessible, but it was an elusive peak, and we never saw it clearly again. Beyond this was the big white peak which had caught our fancy on the march, but from our pass we could only see the lower part of its west ridge.

Prompt and officious as usual, the clouds arrived and the Jugal Himal closed down for the day. Philosophically, we turned downhill. Monica had unroped to take off her *anorak* and forgot to rope up again. Mingma nudged Ang Temba with barely suppressed guffaws. The sight of the memsahib who was most insistent on the use of the rope, heading dreamily for the only hard pitch of the day without it, was too much for him.

It is only just to say that apart from this lapse, Monica was alert and showed presence of mind when climbing. But in London I have known her to walk past her own house when taking me home for a meal and more than once she has remembered too late, on a mountain, that she was having friends for lunch.

When we got back to camp, Kusung greeted us with cheerful salaams and on the spur of the moment added with exaggerated respect, " Salaam, Ang Temba," bowing low and catching this joker without a ready answer. Ang Temba was always teasing Kusung, and we were delighted to see the old man score for once.

For the next few days the snow fell heavily. Monica argued that the monsoon current had set in and no improvement in the weather could be expected, but Mingma kept insisting that we should have a better spell soon. Meantime, we were confined to camp.

There was still plenty to do, however. Photographs to caption, diaries to write, weather signs to be optimistically interpreted.

We could not always write the captions on the spot when taking a picture, and we drew on our invention more than we realised to make up the requisite number. A picture of Kusung struggling to blow up an air-bed, for example, and holding it under his arm like a set of bagpipes might be matched with the words, " We were looking at something no one had ever seen before. The sight was breath-taking and brought tears to our eyes."

The keeping of a diary was a great trial to me because I let it get behind, but Monica kept an up-to-the-minute record and, when we were climbing, left great stains on the snow from a leaky ink bottle as proof of this industry.

A Vital Pass

If it had not been for her, we should never have known the day or the date, a preciseness which was hardly in character.

Time passed in desultory conversation. The most engrossing topic here and in high camps was people, and we discussed friends in some detail, and vied with one another in producing tales about others. Monica seemed to have an unending supply of entertaining or eccentric relatives.

The Sherpas occupied themselves very happily gambling in the " howff." They had a complicated game like monopoly which they played with stones, nails and small blocks of wood, which were arranged all afternoon, according to the throw of the dice. Each throw was accompanied by frenzied patter, a sort of inspired invocation, never twice the same, which culminated in a squeal of triumph or despair. Chhepela and Bahu were the most inveterate gamblers, but Mingma did not take the game seriously at all.

The Sherpas had a word game too, numbers, names or even just vowels being intoned, sometimes with parts allotted, sometimes in chorus. We could not make this game out, but they would play it for hours. They were always singing and the tunes all sounded much the same to us, though some were prayers, chanted at break of day, others were songs for the march or comic ballads of Ang Temba's. There was nothing narrow or prudish about the ballads, judging by the roars of laughter which greeted the end of each verse. We noticed that the Sherpas got as much fun out of observing our mannerisms as we did over theirs. They called the fizzy lemonade powder " oops " and when they thought we were not looking mimicked exactly our enthusiastic reception of a pot of tea.

On the evening of May 4th, Lakpa produced his mouth organ, and the Sherpas did a queer shuffling dance in front

131

of the fire with surprisingly little movement to it. Their rhythms were lively enough and like those of Scottish country dancing—indeed Sherpa music had little in common with Indian music. When we reached Kathmandu, the Sherpas made fun of the strains which floated out from Radio Delhi, just as impudent youngsters might do at home.

Nima Lama told us that there was a pass through to Tibet at the head of the Nosem Khola, which was used as a trade route at certain times of year. Lakpa asserted that he had been to Lhasa by this route but our Sherpas, knowing their Lakpa, were sceptical, and under cross-examination he had to modify this to " somewhere in Tibet."

For the first time it cleared completely as darkness fell. The stars sparkled frostily and we knew the next day would be fine. Sherpas may not be infallible weather prophets but this time Mingma was dead right.

Phurbi Chyachu rose to her full stature, towering above still, misty wreaths in all her queenliness. Behind her the sky changed imperceptibly from pale blue, shot with sunset colourings, to the dark blue of night. The moon rose over the lower hills and its light, flooding the sky, glanced off her polished mail of ice. In front of her danced our homely sparks in unregarded homage. She was superb.

Conversation flowed, with long companionable silences intervening. We were all very cheerful, since it was almost certain we could be off next day again at last.

Only one thing made us anxious. Would Kusung be fit to come? Evelyn had sounded his chest with her stethoscope in the afternoon (thus increasing his prestige enormously) and had diagnosed a chronic cough.

" He'll be all right once he gets up into the mountains again," said Mingma.

That was very much how we felt, too.

132

PART TWO

by Monica Jackson

CHAPTER NINE

We Return to the Attack

ON THURSDAY, the 5th of May, we left base camp to make our second sortie up the great Phurbi Chyachumbu glacier. The previous trip had been purely " *dekhna ka waste*," that is, exploratory. This time we meant business. We had two main objectives: one, to reach the col on the frontier ridge from which we had turned back before; and two, to climb if possible the shapely peak to the west of the low col at the head of the glacier. Other more tentative plans included an attempt on the north peak of Phurbi Chyachu. Actually we had decided that the whole north ridge of this mountain, as seen from base camp, looked as if it might " go," but it was clearly a tremendously long ridge, needing many camps and far more Sherpas and climbers than we could provide. An ascent of the north peak would prove whether or not we were correct in our surmise.

We rose at 4.30 that morning, with fervent prayers for good weather. By sunrise the whole camp was astir, with everyone intent on last-minute tasks. The main preparations had, of course, been made the day before. Betty had worked out the food down to the last raisin; ropes, crampons, pitons and route-marking flags had been packed; boots dubbined; rucksacks made ready. But to-day the high-altitude tents had to be rolled up and stowed in the bags, the Primuses and kitchen gear packed and various minor decisions to be made. Mingma had asked if Bahu might come up the glacier with us this time to supplement Kusung, since he was not very fit. We had suggested to Kusung that he stay at base camp instead, but he assured us vehemently and indignantly that he was well-rested and quite fit to go up again. Evelyn could not find much wrong with him, so we agreed. Bahu had little previous experience of snow- and ice-climbing, but he was very strong and, after all, he *was* a Sola Khombu Sherpa. The difficulty was to find sufficient clothing and equipment for him, and our own slender supplies were drawn upon. Betty and Evelyn gave him spare socks and a pair of snow goggles, and I provided gloves. He already had excellent boots with vibram soles, spoil from one of the big expeditions.

The two Tempathang Sherpas were to accompany us to Camp I and then return to base. Lakpa had bought a pair of boots from one of our climbing Sherpas (who already had better ones than we had been able to provide) and now needed socks to go with them. Wearing the same heart-rending expression which had caused Evelyn to part with a pair of gloves on our previous trip, he sidled up to me and pointed out that his lovely new boots were no use to him without socks. It may have been quite by chance that he approached me first. On the other hand it is true that I had told Murari the evening before, that Lakpa strongly resembled my small son in appearance. Anyway, he was given his socks, albeit somewhat unwillingly. The other Sherpa lad, who was Nima Lama's son, deputising for him in his absence, possessed neither Lakpa's charm nor his cheek. He was content with a cast-off pair of canvas hockey-boots.

The weather was bright and clear and looked set fair. But in spite of this Ang Droma was instructed to light a little votive fire on a rock in the hope—we supposed—of currying favour with the spirits of the mountains. All the same there was a general, if illogical, feeling that this trip would be a successful one, and an air of cheerful expectancy was abroad.

At ten minutes to eight we set off. Three memsahibs, Mingma, Ang Temba, Chhepala, Kusung and Bahu, with Lakpa and the other boy as supernumaries. The march to Camp I was the usual long grind. Once more we scrambled over scree and boulder-hopped until we reached the steep snow slopes. Here we sank thigh-deep in new and not particularly cohesive snow, and began to wonder rather anxiously if we had, after all, been wise to return so soon after the storm. The two ugly gullies were more rotten and ruinous than ever, but once again our footholds held miraculously, and soon we were slithering down loose soft snow towards the moraine.

As we neared camp we saw that a big avalanche had come to within a few feet of the tent we had left pitched there. We had to cross its debris to reach the camp, and we did so to the sound of rocks and ice crashing down from the heights above us. " Dear old Camp I," we said to each other affectionately. " It hasn't changed its character at all." The only difference was that the snow was about two feet deeper and that it was softer and wetter. The tent had collapsed under the weight of it. Ang Temba promptly crawled in and began to bounce off the snow. The sight of the animated folds of canvas heaving and bulging was somehow irresistibly funny and the whole expedition, easily amused at the best of times, came to a standstill, leaning on ice-axes and shouting with laughter. Ang Temba was a true humorist, with an infallible instinct for the comic. His jokes were simple as a rule, but they had a delightful spontaneity, and we found especially endearing the fact that he always laughed so heartily at them himself. One of his favourite games was connected with our evening meal, which he usually brought to us in our tents. The thing was to make us take some more on our plates after we had said " enough." If he could succeed in getting us to empty the pan he felt he had scored a point, but the biggest joke of all was to put another spoonful on the plate of anyone who was not looking. He always accompanied this action with many gestures enjoining silence on the onlookers. (As a matter of fact, this game partly stemmed from the Sherpas' solicitude for our well-being. Used to the vast appetite of the Western male in the mountains, they were convinced that we did not eat enough.)

Another genial pastime of Ang Temba's was imitating people, and at any moment he would be liable to give an impromptu impersonation of someone. One day I gave him my camera to hold. He immediately began to impersonate a memsahib taking photographs and apparently having some difficulty with both camera and subject. This act was very well received by one and all, but in Chhepala's opinion something was missing. At base camp I generally wore a bright cotton scarf on my head, tied peasant-fashion under my chin. Chhepala quietly reached for the checked dish-cloth and gave it to Ang Temba, who put it on in exactly the way I always wore it. Everyone went into gales of laughter, including the court jester himself, overcome as usual by his own wit.

We sent back the Tempathang boys as soon as we arrived, because the wretched clouds had come up again and it had begun to snow. As usual, the promise of the morning had not been fulfilled. Worse, it was still very warm, the monsoon current having strengthened perceptibly during our sojourn at base camp. We feared that the glacier would become highly dangerous if the temperature ceased to drop below freezing-point at nights. The hollow which we had used as a lavatory now showed itself in its true character as a snow-filled crevasse which was thawing fast, so that we took our lives in our hands every time we retired there. But it was the only cover within reach which was safe from falling rocks and ice. The delicate problem of obtaining privacy without risk was one which we had to solve anew at every camp. The Sherpas could not have been more gentlemanly about the whole thing and always looked the other way if they saw any of us retiring in a purposeful manner. But sometimes we had to retire a long way to get out of sight, which, at high altitudes, we resented very much. Fortunately, the question of going out into the bitter cold at night was solved once and for all quite early on, by my firm decision to acquire what I called a " widdling tin." This plan appealed to my friends so greatly that in a very short time we had two widdling tins —one for each tent.

A short recce of the route up the ice-fall proved that our good big steps, though snow-filled, still existed. There was nothing to do now but retire to our tents to sit out the afternoon snowfall. Our sleeping-bags had got wet in transit, and, while we ate and talked, we sat hopefully on the wet patches with the idea of blotting up the moisture into our trousers and drying them off with body heat. Our wet socks we had placed as usual inside the inner bags. Here again the idea was to use body-heat for drying, and it worked up to a point. But there are few things more uncomfortable than a sleeping-bag full of wet socks, except, perhaps, the presence of a pair of climbing-boots placed there to prevent them from freezing. (Not that this precaution prevented them from freezing anyway, at the high camps!)

Inside the memsahibs' tents—and no doubt in the Sherpas' also—the afternoon scene was always one of picturesque squalor. There were the snow-covered boots by the tent door; the sugar spilling out of a Polythene bag;

a bottle of ink disastrously affected by altitude leaking over an already undecipherable diary; sardines balanced on the blades of sheath-knives passing from hand to hand. A note of good cheer would be introduced now and again by Ang Temba's voice outside—" Memsahib—Tea? Coffee? Ovo-tea? (Sherpa for Ovosport), Horli'? Orange Ju'? " As he chanted the names of these beverages his voice would go farther and farther up the scale. Once when Betty hesitated over her choice, he ended on a final squeak, " Rakhsi? " Needless to say there was no rakhsi in the camp at that time.

The gloom of the weather outside was intensified by the gloom of the literature we had brought with us. Betty was reading Moravia's *Woman of Rome*, Evelyn, a Scott Fitz-gerald, and I had Balzac's *Old Goriot*. From these chronicles of unrequited love our attention was frequently distracted by the roar of avalanches and the crash of rockfall outside. But we had grown accustomed to these sounds at Camp I and they had ceased to trouble us overmuch. They certainly did not prevent us sleeping peacefully.

The next morning we climbed the ice-fall on two ropes, Betty leading the first and I the second. To our relief the snow was good and stayed frozen long enough to enable us to climb quickly and confidently. By this time we knew intimately every move on the route which had at first seemed to us so intricate. We all shinned up and down séracs and jumped crevasses with an ease born of familiarity. All, that is, except Bahu. It is interesting to note that though he was a strong and active young man, he made heavy weather of his first trip up the ice-fall. This was partly because he did not know what to expect, but also because he was afraid, and frequently had to be hauled up or over obstacles, squeaking with alarm. However, it did not take him long to get over his initial distrust of steep snow and ice. For was he not a Sherpa from Sola Khombu?

We Return to the Attack

By the time we had reached the upper glacier it was extremely hot and the whole party began to suffer from glacier lassitude. We plodded on and up until we came to a place just below our previous Camp II. Here we unroped and rested, passing the water-bottles filled with lemon drink from hand to hand, and sharing out mint cake and chocolate. Then Chhepala, Kusung and Bahu, leaving their loads, roped up again and went off down the glacier, singing, to bring up the remaining food boxes from Camp I. The rest of us continued up the glacier. We went very slowly, as the sun was now extremely fierce, and for the first time we were anxious for the afternoon clouds (which were following us up the glacier) to overtake us. I was leading and complained afterwards that I had been suffering from indigestion and had found the task of breaking steps an unduly heavy one. But I got no sympathy. Having been high before, I was very little affected by altitude, and was so fit that the others felt it to be only just that I should be a little indisposed occasionally. Besides, people following me through deep snow were not free from trouble themselves. I was so light that however hard I stamped everyone else sank down through my footsteps. On this particular day I was not stamping very hard.

We had decided to make for two conspicuous boulders which lay on the glacier some way below our previous Camp III. When we reached them we made camp, calling it IIA. As soon as the tents were pitched, Mingma and Ang Temba returned for the loads left by the other Sherpas. We felt conscience-stricken over this, as we sheltered from the snow in our tents, but Betty was the only one who did anything about it. She shovelled snow into a pan, lit the Primus, and had tea ready for the Sherpas when they returned. They were delighted, and our stock soared.

CHAPTER TEN

The Frontier Ridge

IT WAS a cold and windy night, and in the morning the
wind still drummed at the tent walls, sending down
upon us icy showers of the frozen condensation of our breath.
Sunlight reached the mountains on the western side of the
glacier at about six, and within an hour the first avalanches
of powder snow had begun to slide down their flanks like
sugar from a caster. But our camp lay nearer the eastern
side, under the cold shadow of the north ridge of Phurbi
Chyachu, and we had to wait an unconscionably long time
for the sun to come and drive out the numbing cold. Meanwhile we forced our feet into half-frozen boots, lacing them
with many pauses to blow on our aching fingers; warmed
our hands again, gratefully, on mugs of hot, sweet, Ovotea,
and then addressed ourselves painfully to the daily chore of
coating our faces, necks and ears with glacier cream and
our lips with another special cream. This entailed sitting
on the tubes until they were sufficiently thawed to be
squeezable, and then patiently spreading the almost solid
cream, which was always frozen to the consistency of
plasticine, over every square inch of skin liable to be exposed
to the destructive ultra-violet rays of the sun at high altitudes. Any area of skin accidentally left uncoated would
be blistered by the end of the day. Our lips always had to
be re-smeared several times before the clouds came up, as

the cream tended to get licked off. As we got higher we found that even the inside of our lips had to be covered with cream to prevent them blistering when we panted.

As soon as Ang Temba and Chhepala saw us doing this, they came along with their little mirrors for a share of the cream. They were lighter in colour than the other Sherpas, and there was not sufficient pigment in their skins to protect them fully. Their faces used to get quite painfully sunburnt until they hit upon the idea of using our cream.

We planned now to make quite sure of reaching the higher col on the frontier ridge the following day, before the clouds came up. We would carry our next camp as high as possible, preferably to the glacier shelf right under the last sharp slope leading to the crest of the ridge, at the point where we had turned back before. To get it done in one lift, we decided to file (temporarily) two of the food boxes, and accordingly parked them in the lee of one of the big boulders.

When we were all ready to start, the perennial rope controversy arose once more. From the beginning we had insisted on roping up on all climbs where a fall would have proved fatal, and especially on glaciers. The Sherpas hated this discipline. Even Mingma himself, though a fine climber, would, if left to himself, often have preferred to take quite unjustifiable risks rather than go to the trouble of tying on the rope. Sometimes, too, his judgment of ice and snow conditions was poor, as he was liable to err on the optimistic side. We found that our Sherpas were on the whole great trusters to luck. We, on the other hand, did our best to counteract this trait by leaving as little as possible to chance. Until now we had always adhered unyieldingly to our roping policy, but to-day we relented for the first time. It was quite true, as Mingma lost no time in pointing out, that the snow was hard frozen this morning, and that the route to the steep ice-slope we had climbed before lay first over the smoothest part of the glacier, and then along a small medial moraine. We were ready in good time, and, it really was safe enough. We decided not to carry our insistence on roping to absurd lengths. So, feeling a little guilty, but also delightfully untrammelled, we all set off at our own pace over the crisp snow surface of the glacier.

To her unbounded joy, vociferously expressed, Evelyn was still feeling fit, though she was now a great deal higher than the point where altitude sickness had overtaken her previously. It was a tremendous relief to her that she had been able to push her ceiling up. I had recovered my form, but to-day it was Betty's turn to feel unwell. " I felt dizzy," she wrote later in her diary, " and there was a gentle swishing in my ears which the others would not oblige me by admitting to in theirs. . . ." However, she said nothing of this at the time and bravely trudged on after us.

The sun blazed down and we moved as fast as we could, so as to get off the glacier before it became unsafe, and up the ice-slope before its snow covering became unstable.

After a while Mingma and Ang Temba shed their loads and made a detour to collect the spare rope, the crampons and the small store of food which we had cached at Camp III on our previous trip. The other three Sherpas came on slowly—very slowly, stopping every now and then to rest and get their breath back. Evelyn and I went ahead to kick steps, making a staircase for the laden Sherpas up the steep ice-slope—now covered by a good layer of firm snow. Much too firm we thought it, for each step required at least three hard kicks, which was no fun at all at that altitude. In fact it was very strenuous work indeed, though we took it turn and turn about.

The step-making became slower and slower as we climbed

higher, and breathing became more difficult. Whenever we stopped and got our breath back we felt strong and energetic, but as soon as we started again every step was an effort. After we had been doing this for nearly three hours we saw Mingma following us up the steps, carrying on his back his big basket of kitchen gear, topped with his own rucksack. He must have climbed fast to catch us up, but he must also have been tired, because he did not offer to take his turn at leading, as he usually did.

By this time the clouds were swirling round us, blotting out the splendour of the mountain scene. The dazzling snow, the black rock and the blue ice, the threadlike line of steps reeling away down the slope behind us, all disappeared in grey vapour. The only colour left was in the little holes made in the snow by the points of our ice-axes, which were still blue as the ice itself. We went on up till we came to the top of a steep rise, which we recognised as being not far from where we had turned back before. There we stopped to rest and have a drink from the water-bottles and share raisins and sweets. Then Mingma and I, leaving rucksack and load behind, went on up to choose a camp-site. Without a weight to carry, even going uphill was much easier, and we quickly mounted into the mist above. We climbed up another slope, which had required crampons last time but was snow-covered now, and so reached the brink of a hollow which lay between the spot where we had turned back before and the foot of the last steep rise which led to the crest of the frontier ridge. We had to wait till the mist lifted a bit before we could see anything. But when it did we went down into the hollow, skirting two biggish crevasses, and found a good camp-site. We stopped there for a while talking over plans for the next two days. Mingma was doubtful about the mountain we were after and did not think we had a hope of getting up

Phurbi Chyachu. He thought the steep subsidiary glacier, coming from the high peaks on the frontier ridge west of the Phurbi Chyachumbu, might prove more rewarding. I privately thought it had looked terrible. Anyway, there was nothing for it but to wait for the morning, when we hoped to get a good look at everything, so we descended again at a run to rejoin Betty and Evelyn, and a few minutes later we all reluctantly picked up our burdens and slowly plodded on again.

Half an hour later we were joined at the camp-site by the other Sherpas and pitched the tents just as it started to snow. The sleeping-bags were all wet again. As soon as Ang Temba discovered this he gathered us round him and pulled them out dramatically one after another from their kitbag. We played up with groans of mock dismay as each came out damper than the last, thus sending him into ecstasies of merriment. The afternoon at Camp IIIA, as we christened it, passed between reading, sleeping, writing up diaries, and doing some running-repairs on our blistered faces. Supper, which was served by Ang Temba with his usual verve, consisted of the inevitable packet-soup, followed by meat bar and dried vegetable stew, followed by stewed prunes and cocoa. We were quite pleased with ourselves at being able to eat all this, as we believed at the time that this camp was at an altitude of very nearly 20,000 feet. Since we had no altimeter, we judged this from contour lines on the map and from Mingma's insistence that he always knew by his physical symptoms at what altitude he was, and that he was now at about 20,000 feet. But the map was far from accurate and, though one hesitates to make sweeping statements, we did feel that Mingma's symptoms might not prove infallible either. We think now that this camp was not higher than 19,000 feet.

That night Betty woke to see the moon shining through

the canvas of the tent. She crawled out of her sleeping-bag and unzipped the door to look out. Before her, gleaming in the moonlight, stood the silent peaks that ringed the head of the great glacier. Unnamed they were, and unclimbed, —perhaps unclimbable—and few of them were marked on the map. In the moonlight they looked strangely shrunken, but more inimical than ever. Still, the clear night and the great cold augured well for the next day. Encouraged, she crept back into her sleeping-bag and fell asleep again.

The morning dawned splendidly, a dazzle of white and gold. We rose and ate early and were ready to start soon after seven. The last steep slope between us and the top of the ridge, which had previously glinted with ice, was now covered with hard-frozen snow and rose alluringly a few yards from our tents. Betty had quite recovered, and Evelyn, who from her tent had been subjecting the party to a running commentary on the progress of her preparations, punctuated her remarks with frequent chants of " I'm feeling fine, I'm feeling fine." This time there was no argument—we blithely left the rope behind. The slope was steep and the effects of altitude soon split the party in two, Evelyn and Betty climbing at their own pace, and I scampering after Mingma, who had plunged into the lead. (There was a certain amount of tacit rivalry between the sirdar and me. He was the fitter of the two, and well he knew it, but he liked to challenge me to races which he always won, to his undisguised pleasure.) I had had a pain in the night, caused by over-eating, I expect. But as soon as we started I was in very good form with my wind perfect and felt like running up the slope behind Mingma. At the top I came alongside and kept up with him easily, though he was full of excitement and going fast. We found ourselves on a beautiful smooth hump-backed col, with an ice-dome topped by a comb of crumbling rocks on our left hand and the terrific cornices, ice-pinnacles and rock spires of the north ridge of Phurbi Chyachu on our right. The col was wide and at first we could see nothing in front of us but blue, blue sky. We hastened forward full of surmise and suddenly saw some rocks ahead. Mingma said, with disappointment, "*Aur pahar* (more mountains) memsahib." But as we came over the curve of the ridge and began to descend (into Tibet, I suppose) we realised that the rocks were nothing but a pair of isolated rock pinnacles, like the frame of a sort of window, with a mass of broken slaty rocks between them, forming a ledge. Below this the ridge fell away in a sheer precipice into Tibet. To the right of the pinnacles the precipice was an almost perpendicular ice-fall, to the left of them it was a perpendicular ice couloir. As we hurried towards the rocks we came to some snow-covered crevasses. Mingma said, "*Hath do* (give me your hand), memsahib." I did so and hand-in-hand, like children, we walked towards the ledge saying, "Tibet, Tibet." When we reached it, we sat down (our feet dangling in the air of Tibet), and divided our attention between the marvellous view and the charming spectacle of a flock of snow pigeons wheeling about below us, until Betty and Evelyn came up.

It was now clear to us that, unlike the Langtang, the Jugal Himal has a frontier ridge which is very sharp and well-defined. Quite astonishingly so, in fact. The mountains on the ridge have all their bulk in front, on the Nepal side—ridges, buttresses, snowfields and hanging glaciers—and nothing at all behind on the Tibetan side. From its crest the ridge drops straight down into Tibet, not gradually or in steps, but vertically. The impression one gets from a viewpoint on the ridge itself is that some of the mountains are almost two-dimensional, like stage scenery, and, indeed, as seen in profile, they seem to consist entirely of narrow and tortuous arêtes. From the Tibetan side this great wall of ice and rock must present an extraordinarily impressive sight. The bare hills of Tibet, range upon range of them, were purple and brown and rolled away into the distance. To the north-west was a hint of broad plains beyond, but to the north-east was a great tangle of mountains which were not marked on the map at all. Where they should have been was a large blank marked " unsurveyed." Thousands of feet below us lay an alp with frozen lakes on it, and farther away still we could see a river valley. In this valley, but hidden from us, lay the Tibetan frontier-post of Nyenam, manned, we had been told, by Chinese Communists. We had been warned against crossing over into their territory. However, except perhaps at this one broad col, where we may technically have been a few yards over the frontier as we sat on the ledge, there was no likelihood of our wandering by mistake out of the Jugal Himal and trespassing. The only way of getting properly into Tibet from any of the points we reached on the frontier would have been to *fall* in.

Having gazed our fill at the forbidden land, we turned our attention to the " Ladies " Peak we had hoped to climb. We now saw that it would be very, very difficult, and was quite impossible to reach from where we stood. It fell away extremely steeply on the north and south from a long knife-edge ridge, heavily corniced, and appeared quite out of the question for loaded climbers.

Disappointed, we turned our eyes eastward for yet another wincing glance at the appalling start to the north ridge of Phurbi Chyachu. What a mountain! Its pinnacles of ice and rock leaned away from each other at fantastic angles. " Like a grotesque flower opening," as Betty put it. We averted our eyes hastily. Phurbi Chyachu was not for us.

But Ang Temba, who had come up with Betty and Evelyn, felt the need to make a gesture of defiance. He set off smartly across the col and up the ridge, carrying one of our route-marking flags, until his further progress was barred by the first ice-wall. There he stuck in the flag, like an urchin cocking a snoot at a duchess, and returned in triumph. We sympathised heartily, but unfortunately we thought we might need the flag again. He was sent back to retrieve it.

While Betty remained on the ledge (wrapped in ecstatic contemplation and ignoring the mute reminders of duty which lay around her in the form of binoculars, prismatic compass, exposure meter, and a variety of lenses and filters) Evelyn, Mingma and I recrossed the col to have a look at the mountains to the west of the one we had hoped to climb. Almost at once we saw a possibility—perhaps it would be more truthful to say the *only* possibility. This was a mountain which had a long gentle slope of pure blue ice running up to a domed summit. Compared with its companions, nearly all of which seemed frankly impossible, this one looked inoffensive—almost welcoming. But it also looked rather inaccessible. It stood farther north than any of the others, which was why it had been invisible, or nearly so, from the main glacier. The only way to reach it was to climb a difficult glacier which we had hitherto disregarded because we had not cared for the look of it. Beyond this mountain again rose a fine cone of snow and ice, which we recognised as the big white peak to the north of Dorje Lakpa. It had no name, but was marked on the map as being over 23,000 feet high. It was the highest mountain in the Jugal Himal, and it was the only other peak in the whole area which looked possible. But we were pretty sure that it would be too much for an expedition as small as ours, as it would require supporting camps, for which we had neither the equipment nor the requisite number of climbers and Sherpas.

Mingma pointed to the domed summit and said, " That is a good mountain, memsahib. Why don't we climb that? It is much higher than this other with the narrow ridge."

Translating his comments, I added, heavily sarcastic, " And of course we reach it by climbing that glacier, skilfully dodging the avalanches as we go."

" That glacier " was the difficult one leading to the peak, the one Mingma had hinted at in his conversation with me the day before. We had looked across at it from camp that morning with growing interest, but we had not seriously considered it as a possibility until now. It fell to the Phurbi Chyachumbu from the big white peak and the domed mountain and was pretty steep. Its lower half was an ice-fall, and on its true right it was swept by avalanches from the great peak which rose above it on that side. On its true left, or northern side, was a kind of snow corridor which at first sight looked like the key to its relatively smooth upper half. But this corridor was also threatened with avalanche, being overhung in places by ice cornices. The centre part of the glacier was fairly safe from avalanche danger, but it was criss-crossed with huge crevasses. This glacier was Y-shaped, and bifurcated under a buttress of the big white peak. One arm ran north behind the domed mountain. We thought it must fall from a high col on the frontier ridge. The other arm ran south-west to a col which looked very much as if it would prove to be a pass leading over to the head of the Dorje Lakpa glacier. If we *did* succeed in forcing a way up the steep ice-fall to the smoother, though still steep, slopes of the upper glacier, we would be able to camp at the junction of the Y. It then remained to be seen whether or not it would be necessary to place a still higher camp on or just below the frontier ridge, from which to make the final assault on our mountain. From a camp at the junction of the Y it should also be possible to climb up to the col overlooking the Dorje Lakpa glacier to ascertain whether or not it was a true pass.

Evelyn announced that in her opinion the middle of the glacier was quite safe from avalanche. We agreed. But the problem would be to find a way through the gaping crevasses which honeycombed the centre part of the ice-fall. They looked formidable even from a distance. Nevertheless, we began to point out to each other possible ways of circumventing them. We had talked ourselves into the right mood of optimism. Highly elated, we hurried back to Betty and Ang Temba, who had returned, no whit chastened, with the flag.

It was now imperative, the Sherpas said, to build a cairn. " Because," as Mingma pointed out, " Nobody has ever been here before us." There was plenty of material lying about for it, as the whole ledge consisted of a jumble of loose slates. We all helped, but the Sherpas were the architects, with the result that in the end the cairn turned out to be a very handsome *chorten*. We thought it was a far better idea to have built a *chorten* in humble thanksgiving to the lord Buddha rather than a cairn in mere self-advertisement.

Mingma and Ang Temba then climbed one of the crazy pinnacles and, in a regrettable spirit of bravado, built another chorten on top of it. Evelyn and I regarded the rock with mistrust and made no attempt to follow them. But Betty went up after the Sherpas. The rock was quite rotten—the sort of thing one climbs in nightmares—so, having courageously asserted the right of a memsahib to live as dangerously as a Sherpa, she did not hang about with them on the summit, but beat a dignified retreat. It had

Packing equipment in a Glasgow warehouse in preparation for the expedition.

These temples congregate in the open squares of Kathmandu. They seemed to show a Chinese influence, but the citizens themselves deny this.

Monica and Evelyn beside the first chortens on the march. These show
that we were nearing a Buddhist village.

Monica and Betty sorting gear
in camp on the march in.

Crossing a swing bridge on the march in.

Porters following the track through the lower gorges of the Balephi Khola. This is the " main road " to Tempathang from Kathmandu.

Evelyn paying off the Nepali porters at Tempathang.

Tensing Lama, one of the Tempathang men, signs on with his thumbprint.

Our climbing Sherpas. From left to right: Ang Temba, Chhepela, Kusung and Mingma.

Bridging the Rakhta Khola. There was no question of wading this swift and violent torrent.

Ang Droma, our sixteen-year-old sherpani who carried a fifty pound load without complaining.

At base camp, Chhepela makes chupattis and watches the pressure cooker, while Mingma darns his trousers.

The Phurbi Chyachumbu glacier. The icefall in the foreground is the one we first climbed.

View of Phurbi Chyachu ridge from a high col between Nepal and Tibet.

Betty, Evelyn, Mingma and Ang Temba, with the chorten we built on the Frontier Ridge.

From a framework of rock pillars on the Frontier Ridge, we looked into Tibet. We could see many peaks in this closed land, unclimbed, unnamed and unattainable.

View of Ladies' Glacier and Gyalgen Peak.

Monica and Evelyn looking up at Ladies' Glacier.

Looking back at Phurbi Chyachu, which forms part of the Frontier Ridge, from Camp IV, half-way up Ladies' Glacier.

Climbing upper crevassed area, Ladies' Glacier.

Mingma is leading a rope through the upper icefall on the Ladies' Glacier. We were aiming for a snow corridor on the right, where we had to keep at a respectful distance from avalanche tracks.

Negotiating the overhang on the far side of the great crevasse.

View of the lower icefall of the Dorje Lakpa glacier from above base camp.

Gyalgen, Monica and Ang Temba on the summit of Gyalgen Peak.

Monica looking at Dorje Lakpa glacier.

Sherpa women in Tempathang. Their hair glistens from the yak butter they use as a conditioner.

On the march out, Evelyn looks down on Panch Pokhari, a holy place of five lakes near Tempathang.

Betty washes her hair in one of the Panch Pokhari lakes, where the Indrawati River has its source.

now become very cold. The wind blew in chill gusts across the col and the mountains of Tibet buried themselves in cloud. It was time to descend. On the way we stopped to enlist Betty's sympathy for our new plan. She fell in with it enthusiastically, and the whole party returned to camp in a very exalted frame of mind.

There was nobody at the tents but Chhepala asleep in the sun. Kusung and Bahu had gone down to fetch the food boxes from Camp IIA. Since our plans had been changed there was now no need for this, and Chhepala was dispatched post-haste to recall them. The rest of us had tea, biscuits and our midday sardines, and rejoiced to see that the afternoon clouds were mounting in a very half-hearted manner and looked as if they might blow away altogether. Later, Mingma and Ang Temba came back from a short excursion out of sight, which we had modestly refrained from joining, with the news that they had found a quicker way down—a steep but practicable snow couloir which debouched on to the main glacier.

Time passed, the clouds came and went, and it was warm enough to sit out on our air-mattresses, to write up diaries, work on photograph captions and pore over map and compass readings. Meanwhile, there was no sign of the three Sherpas. We began to think that Chhepala must have misunderstood his instructions and that they had all gone back to Camp IIA to wait for us. This is, in fact, just what had happened. Mingma, feeling a little guilty at not having been sufficiently explicit, dutifully set off on the long, long trek to fetch them back.

The clouds lifted completely as the afternoon wore on. This was the first clear afternoon we had been granted since reaching base camp, and we greatly appreciated it. We felt that it was all that was needed to complete a singularly happy and memorable day—a flawless day, for which the labour and exertion of all the past weeks and months seemed a small price to pay.

Ang Temba now began to get anxious about Mingma's prolonged absence. He paced about restlessly, kicking empty tins into crevasses and scurrying from one observation post to another in the hope of catching sight of the returning men. Eventually we began to feel worried too. It was getting late. But at last, Ang Temba, who had gone to see whether by any chance the Sherpas might have decided to return up the newly discovered couloir, gave a shout of relief. We hastened to join him and found him standing much too near the edge of a huge snow cornice overhanging the main glacier. We drew him back with remonstrances which he joyously disregarded, saying, " There, there they are," and giving the shrill, far-carrying Sherpa whistle. There came a faint answering echo. He pointed across the glacier and at last we saw, far below and right away at the foot of the ice-fall we proposed to climb the following day, a line of dots. It was Mingma and two of the Sherpas. Through the field-glasses we could see that they had sensibly roped up and that they had a food box with them. Mingma had been all the way back to Camp IIA, it transpired, and then had a brainwave. Why not deposit one of the boxes at the foot of to-morrow's climb? He took Chhepala and Bahu, leaving Kusung, who was tired, to climb back alone to Camp IIIA by our route of the previous day.

We watched them come back across the glacier, and then creep slowly up the long couloir towards us. As they neared the top, Kusung came into camp with dragging feet and bowed head, too weary to respond with his usual cheerful smile to our shouted greetings. The other Sherpas climbed over the lip of the couloir soon after, and we welcomed them with congratulations and tea. They grinned broadly, delighted to find themselves the heroes of the hour.

CHAPTER ELEVEN

The Unknown Glacier

O N THE morning of the 9th of May we packed up and left Camp IIIA, descending by the snow couloir and striking westward across the main glacier to the foot of the ice-fall. When we reached the place where the Sherpas had left the box the previous evening, we stopped to confer and reorganise. It was decided that Evelyn, as the most likely to be affected by altitude higher up, should lead the first rope to-day, and Betty the following day, keeping me in reserve for the third day in case the other two should have reached their ceiling by then. This arrangement gave each of us responsibility in turn and worked out very well in practice. On this day Evelyn started off with Betty, Mingma and Chhepala. Leading the second rope I followed with Kusung, Ang Temba and Bahu.

The glacier began as it meant to go on, tilting steeply upward with an air of no nonsense about it. The sun was hot and the snow rather soft. Kusung, who was clearly still unfit, very soon started to wilt. Every few minutes Ang Temba would call out to me, " Memsahib, *kole, kole.*" This meant " stop " in the Sherpa tongue. I would turn round to see Kusung leaning on his ice-axe and gasping like a landed fish. Progress at this rate was slow and the party on the first rope was a long way ahead. I took off my rucksack, and hunting out a box of glucose tablets, made

Kusung eat two of these, which helped to keep him going for a bit.

Meantime, the party in front had halted below a great upheaval of séracs intertwined with crevasses through which no route was immediately perceptible. The ice pinnacles reared up, capped and caped with sheets of thawing snow which threatened to slide off bodily into the waiting crevasses. It was a place which brought forcibly to mind the well-known dictum that the three most important rules of Himalayan climbing are (1) reconnoitre, (2) reconnoitre, (3) reconnoitre. They stopped to rest, reflect and let our party catch up. When we arrived, Mingma, who had been restraining his impatience with difficulty, quietly unroped and set off to investigate. It took a moment or two for us to realise what he was about, but when it sank in I shouted for him to stop and wait for a rope. There are none so deaf as those who won't hear, and Mingma went on, testing each step ostentatiously with his ice-axe. Ang Temba, who was devoted to Mingma, frenziedly unhitched a rope, dragging the loops unceremoniously over the heads of his comrades and muttering anxiously the while, " He must not go unroped." This was the only time any of the Sherpas was heard to insist on a rope, and the memsahibs could not refrain from unseemly mirth when severity of mien would have been more appropriate. Ang Temba chased after Mingma, bearing the rope and a strongly worded message ordering him back. They returned together, Mingma wearing an expression of injured innocence which quickly dissolved into a mischievous grin when we shook our heads at him. Evelyn tied herself on to keep an admonitory eye on their proceedings, and the three of them set off again to find a way over, or through the obstacles confronting us.

The rest of us settled down to occupy ourselves with

changing films, renewing lip-protection cream and watching through the binoculars the progress of the reconnaissance party. I offered Kusung a drink from my water-bottle, which he needed so badly that by the time he returned it to me with some embarrassment it was nearly empty. He was deeply mortified by his unfitness, and, in a pathetic attempt to salve his wounded pride, he began to talk nostalgically of the good old pre-war days. " I was as strong then as Ang Temba is now," he said in surprisingly good Hindustani, " And my wife, Ang Droma's mother, was equally strong. Shipton Sahib was very pleased with us. In these days," he added, eyeing us reproachfully, " we went to Everest through Tibet, and the sahibs rode to the mountain on ponies and did not carry their own rucksacks." The memsahibs glanced self-consciously at their own rucksacks, which they had also shouldered during the march, and felt thoroughly common. Kusung sighed. The world was not what it was and he had been reduced to slumming.

The reconnaissance party were now creeping like flies up the face of a mighty sérac. They looked exceptionally insecure, and appeared to be choosing a needlessly difficult route. Betty and I, doing a spot of back-seat climbing, shouted, " What's the matter with the other side? " " It's about to *avalanche*," Evelyn's voice came faintly in reply. The three little figures, who looked so far off, but whose voices still reached us clearly, disappeared over the top of the sérac. They went on up, cutting and stamping a route for loaded climbers, until they came to an easier stretch. This route led them more and more to their right as they circumvented one big crevasse after another, until they found themselves in the snow corridor on the true left of the glacier. They looked about suspiciously, but could see no signs of large avalanche tracks. It seemed as if the corridor might be the key after all. On the way up they came suddenly on a line of tracks and Mingma shouted excitedly, " It's a yeti, memsahib. Look! " Evelyn looked, but could not bring herself to believe that these small tracks were those of an abominable snowman. Though what any animal was doing, crossing such inhospitable terrain, was more than she could imagine.

They returned to the main party and told us the story of the yeti tracks. " Only four inches long? They *couldn't* have been yeti tracks, Mingma," I said sceptically. Mingma hesitated, looking nonplussed. Then he brightened. " I think it was an eight-year-old yeti," he announced firmly. The whole party burst out laughing and Mingma looked a little hurt.

We loaded and roped up again, four to a rope, and went slowly on through the ice-fall, now skirting a green ice-cave with a hanging curtain of icicles, now climbing a ladder of steps, now driving in ice-axes to belay each other over a crevasse. When we came to the " yeti tracks " we could make nothing of them. Some animal with longish feet had imprinted a single track across the glacier, marching up and down the séracs. It seemed to be travelling straight from one grim rock wall to another for no reason at all.

We did not linger over the tracks because the clouds were rolling up behind us. How we resented those clouds! Particularly on this glacier where good visibility was an absolute necessity if we were to succeed in climbing the ice-fall. We came at last to the corridor and followed it, now and then craning our necks apprehensively to look up at the rock wall on our right, and wincing at the sight of the cornices far above. The surface of the snow was corrugated with the tracks of small avalanches and their debris was piled up all the way, just where the corridor flattened out before the séracs began. But there were no big avalanche tracks, and we kept to a line between the fringe of debris and the sêracs, where the snow was smooth and unmarked.

At a halt Evelyn suddenly said, " I've done enough. You go ahead, Monica." She was pale and looked unwell. We regarded her with concern. She had eaten little this day or the day before, and the two climbs up the ice-fall in one morning had taken it out of her. We feared that she was approaching a new altitude " ceiling." I said I thought we ought to camp soon, anyway. The clouds were upon us and some of the Sherpas had to return for the food box still sitting at the foot of the ice-fall.

" We can't camp here," Betty put in briefly. " Too dangerous—if a big avalanche came down it would sweep us straight into a crevasse."

This was true. We must look for a safer site farther on. Evelyn decided under the circumstances to stay with her rope and they went on slowly.

Just as our second rope was about to get under way Chhepala in his quiet voice asked Bahu to come back with him to fetch the food box. Bahu refused point-blank, saying that he was not going down there again for anybody. Whereat Kusung sprang to his feet exclaiming contemptuously, " All right. If you dare not, I will go. An old man like me! " We listened, puzzled, to the argument, and I now intervened, asking what was the matter. This was the first time we had ever heard the Sherpas quarrel. They all explained at once.

" Without a rope *nobody* is going back," I said firmly, " and the third rope is packed. You must wait to return till we camp."

" But, memsahib," Chhepala protested in his gentle, reasonable way, " if we do not camp soon it will be a very long way to go back for the load, and it is beginning to snow. Mingma wants to camp *above* the ice-fall to-day."

I unroped, dumped my rucksack, and dashed off after Evelyn's party. Catching them up, I told the sirdar of the argument, adding that the top of the ice-fall was out of the question this day.

"Bahu is inexperienced, and Kusung is not well," Mingma said. "Ang Temba and I will return for the box."

Very well, I agreed, they could. But it would be a long way down and back, even from this point. We did not want our sirdar exhausted before we reached our highest camp. Besides, could he not see that the doctor memsahib had mountain sickness? These arguments appealed to Mingma and he regretfully agreed that he had been over-ambitious. Evelyn decided to rejoin Betty and the other Sherpas, who were just round the corner, while I went on with Mingma and Ang Temba looking for a camp-site. We found one at last which seemed suitable. It was a flat peninsula of the snow corridor, thrusting out into the glacier. Between it and the avalanche tracks gaped a large bergschrund, or side crevasse, which would swallow all but the biggest avalanches. Above were rock cliffs seamed with snow gullies which did not appear to have overhanging cornices. It was not an ideal spot, but it was comparatively safe. Mingma and Ang Temba unloaded and set about stamping out places for tents, while I returned for my rucksack, meeting and passing the rest of the party coming along at their own pace. On my way back I exchanged greetings with Mingma and Ang Temba, hastening down to collect the box. They were going downhill and were unburdened, so they whistled and sang as they went. By the time they returned, covered with snow, camp was made, a recalcitrant Primus had been coaxed into working, and tea was brewed.

That night we all slept soundly except for Betty, whose mountaineer's conscience was an unusually active one. She felt that Camp IV was not absolutely safe, though she realised that there had been no alternative. Every so often she would wake to hear the avalanches roaring down the mountain on the opposite side of the glacier and to shiver involuntarily in her sleeping-bag. But no avalanches came our way.

In spite of Betty's impatience to be away out of the place, it was about 9 a.m. before we left Camp IV. Ours seemed to be the last corner of the glacier to get the morning sun, and in the intense cold our preparations were slow. Evelyn had been able to take little but liquid this morning or the night before and had woken feeling nauseated and with a severe headache. The Sherpas were all huddled in their tents, crouching over the Primuses. We watched, shivering, the edge of the sunlight creeping almost imperceptibly across the glacier towards us. At eight o'clock, when it was high time we left, Mingma cunningly appeared with a kettle, saying soothingly, " Let us all have some tea, Memsahib, till the sun comes. It is a very cold morning." This was more than ardent tea drinkers like Betty and I could resist, and we hastened unashamedly to fetch our mugs. The tea party lasted until a tongue of light and warmth lapped at the frozen shadow in which our snow platform lay, when Sherpas and memsahibs rose with one accord and ran towards it, to warm themselves in it as at a fire.

It was Betty's turn to lead the first rope, followed by Mingma, Chhepala and me. Evelyn led the second rope with Ang Temba, Kusung and Bahu. We all set off along the snow corridor, looking for a way back on to the glacier proper. Forging ahead, Betty's rope was making good time, when, all at once, it came to a standstill. Another line of tracks, coming down from the glacier and showing faintly on the frozen snow, ran diagonally across the corridor. Each narrow footprint was about nine inches long, and the strangest thing about them was that they were at least seven feet apart. We carefully paced the distance between them. "You see? That is without doubt the track of a yeti," Mingma said triumphantly. We were prepared to believe him. We could think of no other explanation, though why even a yeti should wish to go bounding about in this high wilderness of ice and snow was beyond our comprehension.

"Why are there no toe-prints?" we inquired. Mingma gave us a pitying look. "Because they walk with their toes curled in, like this "—he demonstrated with his fingers.

"What do yetis eat?" I asked. Mingma shook his head and said he did not know. Then, reluctant to lose standing as an authority on the natural history of the abominable snowman, he added quickly, "Perhaps things under stones." He went on to say that there were three types of yeti, one as big as a yak, one as big as a man, and one small, like a pygmy. We decided that the tracks at present under review came into the middle category. We photographed them with an ice-axe laid alongside in the classic manner, though we did not think they were clear enough to show up well.

After this we made our way on to the glacier, and Betty led up and down with vigour the swelling waves and sharp crests of snow-covered ice. Some of the crevasses we encountered were immense, their walls striated in layers of different colours—pastel pinks, blues, greens, and creams—like slices of some exotic neapolitan cake. We managed to skirt or cross them all until Betty climbed a last steep sérac, and stopped short at the top. At her feet was the biggest crevasse any of us had ever seen. It seemed to stretch from end to end of the glacier, and her heart sank. But our blood was up, and we were not going to be beaten now if we could help it. Mingma, questing like a hound along the brink of the crevasse, found a breach in its impregnability and hurled himself down through a gap to test it, and we did not protest, but cheered him on and were ready to follow him. At this point the crevasse was choked with debris. Great blocks of ice and snow (" All stuck together," as Betty said, " Like sweeties in a boy's pocket "), had fallen from its upper wall. This debris was, it is true, just a fragile layer with great depth under it, but so early in the day the blocks were frozen together solidly enough. It was certainly worth putting to the test. Already in the lead, Mingma raced across, prodding here, cutting a step there and jumping gaps. The others on his rope followed him, while the second rope awaited a signal to come across. Even so early, the passage afforded by the debris was not very secure. It was full of holes into which legs would slip to the tinkle of ice fragments falling far below, and the crevasse was so wide that the whole party had to be on the " bridge " at the same time. The farther wall barred our egress with a great overhang which had to be cut away, and Mingma flung himself upon it with his ice-axe like a man possessed. After about half an hour of hard and hair-raising battle the crevasse suddenly surrendered and the first party scrambled with relief on to solid ice again. Even so, they had needed to climb out using an awkward chimney technique which meant that all loads had to be removed and hauled up separately.

The second party could now begin to cross, while Betty's party went on to prospect, fearing to encounter another major obstacle. But, though we did come to a last gaping crevasse, we found a beautiful knife-edge of ice, conveniently capped with snow, which ran right across it, forming a narrow tight-rope of a bridge. We returned with the good news to the great crevasse, and the two parties foregathered on the snow just above it, congratulating ourselves and eating jam mixed with snow, a favourite delicacy among the Sherpas.

163

Apart from its size, the most remarkable thing about the great crevasse was the heavenly deep blue of the ice in places. It looked quite unearthly.

The knife-edge was the last obstacle the ice-fall had to offer, and so pleased were we to be over the previous one that we discounted the difficulty of this, and balanced across it, one after another, without a tremor, though the bridge was only a few inches wide and the abyss on either side of it was deep and dark. Once over, we saw the glacier rearing up in front of us, smooth and unblemished. We were up!

But now the hard work really began, as we climbed on and on for several hours, making for the junction of the Y. After Betty had been leading for some time she began to need a rest, and the others on her rope took over the lead in turns, because, now that the snow was soft, this was a very strenuous job, the leader sinking in at every step. The clouds came up, of course, but not before we had seen a possible route up our mountain. It was very long and would have involved endless step-cutting, and probably an exposed camp on the ice-ridge, so we hoped that there *would* be a col at the head of the glacier arm running to the north-west of the mountain, and that there would be a shorter and equally feasible route to the summit from the col.

Betty was still leading when the mist enveloped us, and she found it hard to see where to put her feet. In the white snow and the white mist she needed some dark object upon which to fix her eyes, and, being denied this, reeled drunkenly about until called to order by the climbers behind. Higher up still the clouds thinned again, and as we approached the point where the glacier bifurcated a howling wind, sweeping down from the westerly col, drove them away completely. We found ourselves looking towards

164

a level stretch of snow with a crust polished smooth by the wind, below another monumental ice-fall. Visibility was still not good, because the wind drove before it clouds of powder snow which stung our faces and got into our eyes. But we could just see on our left one arm of the glacier, leading gently up to this col to the west which looked so much like a pass to the head of the Dorje Lakpa glacier. In front of us rose a shoulder of ice and snow, which was a buttress of the big white peak itself—the highest mountain in the Jugal Himal. Slightly right of this was the ice-fall, above which, we now saw, there really was a high col on the frontier ridge. To-morrow we would try to reach it and to climb to our summit from there.

By now it was three o'clock and everyone was very tired. I was taking a turn at leading, stamping steps through unpleasant crusted snow, when Mingma said wearily, " Let us camp here, memsahib." For a moment I was tempted to agree, but the snow still lay at an angle, and there is nothing more uncomfortable than sleeping in a tent pitched on a slope. "Just a little farther," I said, and plodded on, wishing with all my heart that the angle would ease off there and then. But this camp was not to be won easily, and it was some time before we at last reached the level snow. This was a beautiful place for a camp-site, but not a comfortable one, being exposed to a continual gale. However, we had no choice. We had all done enough for one day. Evelyn had recovered as the day went on and had even done some strenuous step-cutting in the great crevasse, but she was at the end of her reserves of strength, while Kusung was grey with fatigue. We pitched the tents with their tails to the wind and got into them as quickly as possible. Evelyn was again incapable of eating and we felt a bit worried about her, though she cheerfully assured us that she would be all right after a night's rest.

Tents in the Clouds

That night there was a violent thunderstorm. The wind screamed over the col to the south-west, lightning glimmered all round us, and thunder clattered among the peaks. The storm retreated down our glacier and we could hear the thunder rumbling away below for a long time. An odd sensation, to hear thunder beneath rather than above one. But we did not savour it for long, falling asleep even while the storm raged. When we woke at intervals later in the night the weather was clear and the moon shining brightly through the canvas of the tents.

CHAPTER TWELVE

Gyalgen Peak

THE WIND was still blowing hard on the morning of the 11th of May, but the day was fine and clear. It was now or never for the domed mountain.

In spite of a good night's rest, we were all rather slow in starting. It was very cold, and little jobs such as lacing boots and putting anti-mist on our snow goggles seemed to consume an inordinate amount of time and energy. In other words, we were feeling the altitude.

Evelyn dressed and went out into the sunshine. She had a pounding headache, but hoped she would feel better when she got moving, as she had done the previous day. At once she was overcome by a violent spasm of nausea and vomited. This attack was followed by a feeling of utter exhaustion, and she realised that altitude sickness had her firmly in its grip. She went slowly back to the tent she had shared with Betty and there after a struggle with herself she came to a difficult decision. She would not try to accompany the assault party for fear of hampering them or keeping them back. When she broke the news to Betty and me we were distressed on her account, but applauded her courage in facing up to the situation. It was going to be a long and strenuous climb even for people who were fit and well fed, and Evelyn had been on a starvation diet for days.

167

Tents in the Clouds

Mingma and Ang Temba were to be the other members of the party, and they were ready by eight o'clock. So was Betty. She looked around for me but I was nowhere to be seen. Her story goes that she discovered me kneeling in my tent, absorbed in putting a film in my camera and murmuring to myself in a sort of chant—" Camera, compass, map, torch, spare socks, silk gloves, wool gloves, windproof mitts. . . ."

" Come on," Betty said reprovingly, " what *are* you doing? "

I replied that I was changing a film, of course, and sorting out gear to take with me. Rather impatiently I suggested that she should go and get ready, as it really was time we left.

" I *am* ready," Betty said, laughing. " We're all waiting for you."

" Oh, are you? " I was mildly surprised. " Come on, then."

Bundling all the essentials I might need for the day into my small rucksack, I crawled out of the tent, reached for my ice-axe and declared myself ready to go. I am convinced that it was either cold or altitude which had so numbed my brain that morning that I was incapable of concentration or consecutive thought until I got moving. But Betty has since been heard to remark that it was all just a piece of Jackson vagueness, such as she had experienced at varying temperatures and at all altitudes, including sea-level.

Our assault party of four now set off, working its way across the glacier and beneath the ice-fall in the hope of finding a loophole in its defences. Sure enough, on the far side, we were able to sneak through what Betty described as " A little backdoor of a crevasse," which we had nevertheless to treat with great respect. The snow varied in quality from bad to worse. Sometimes it had a crust which

168

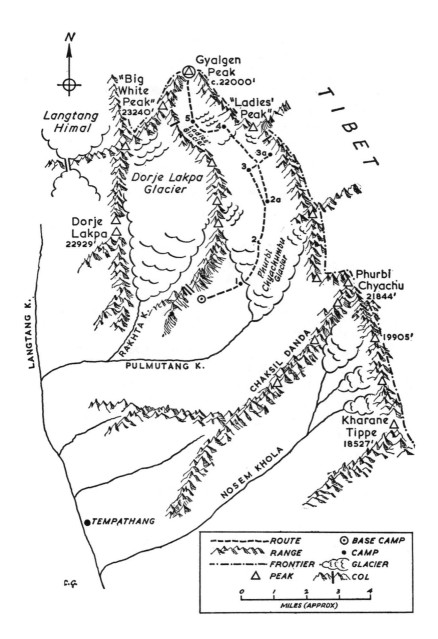

N

Gyalgen
Peak
c. 22000'

"Big
White
Peak"
23240'

Langtang
Himal

"Ladies'
Peak"

T I B E T

5

Ladies'
Glacier

3a

3

Dorje Lakpa
Glacier

2a

Dorje
Lakpa
22929'

2

Phurbi
Chuachumbu
Glacier

Phurbi
Chyachu
21844'

19905'

LANGTANG K.

RAKHTA K.

PULMUTANG K.

CHAKSIL DANDA

Kharane
Tippe
18527'

NOSEM KHOLA

● TEMPATHANG

C. G.

	ROUTE	⊙	BASE CAMP
	RANGE	●	CAMP
	FRONTIER		GLACIER
△	PEAK		COL

0   1   2   3   4

MILES (APPROX)

gave way, not at every step, but just often enough to make rhythmic climbing impossible. At other times it was deep and soft and clung to our boots like clay, so that we had to strike our feet with our ice-axes at every other step to knock off the lumps which weighed them down.

After a time we came to another crevasse, a big one this time, which stretched right across the glacier. We could not turn it on the right, but saw that if we traversed its length along its lower lip we could turn in on the left. This we started to do, and soon found ourselves at the top of a smooth ice-slope with this crevasse on one side and another large crevasse, grinning like a shark, lying in wait below. We had to move softly and delicately, like cats on a roof, our Vibram soles clinging to a fine skin of snow which overlay the ice. Before we reached the end of the crevasse we came to a place where it was snow-filled to the top. Mingma suggested that we should cross here. " I don't think it's safe," I said doubtfully misliking the look of it.

" Oh yes, memsahib, it will be quite safe so early in the day. Look . . ." Mingma prodded the snow with his axe. It appeared to be firm enough. Ang Temba joined his arguments to Mingma's and Betty was too out of breath to vouchsafe any opinion. Still grumbling that I did not like it, I allowed myself to be persuaded, and we made a successful but possibly risky short-cut across the snow covering of the crevasse.

The glacier now reared up sharply, the col at its head looking depressingly high and far away. Patches of blue ice gleamed above us as we began a climb that seemed endless. Mingma, who had led up to the first crevasse, abdicated in favour of Ang Temba and retired to the rear. We had agreed to the Sherpas' leading to begin with, because their greater strength would enable them to make steps through the bad snow without using up all their reserves of energy. Ang Temba stamped out steps with his usual cheerful vigour, and we continued to gain height fast, though at the price of a growing breathlessness which made more and more work for our labouring lungs. Betty writes in her diary with feeling—" Long long slopes went up and up, mostly soft snow with ice showing through unexpectedly. Monica took her turn at leading and step-cutting, but I was feeling the altitude and it was all I could do to follow. I tried every system I could think of to keep going; breathing more quickly than I need; taking two breaths to every step; then three, then four, but all were exhausting. I wanted to cry, but no one would give me time ! "

We stopped at intervals to rest and to observe with interest the way in which mountains we had been used to see towering above us had now begun to shrink. The " Ladies " peak we had originally hoped to climb had crumpled away into a thin jagged outline well below us. Phurbi Chyachu herself (we always thought of this mountain as feminine) now showed up much less impressively, having a distinctly tadpole-like appearance, called to mind by the miles of twisting ridge connected to the round head of her summit. We looked down on the col on which we had stood three days ago, and beyond it saw the massed mountains of Tibet, marching in battalions into the distance.

At one of these pauses Betty recovered her breath enough to say what was in her mind. She was afraid that she was keeping us back. I assured her that she was not, which was true, but she was still unconvinced and extracted a promise that once at the col, Mingma and I would not wait for her but go on to the top of the mountain. Hoping to convince her I turned to Mingma and told him that she had never been in the Himalaya before. Did he not agree that she was going well? To our astonishment, Mingma regarded us solemnly and proceeded to treat us to a minor panegyric on our climbing prowess. He began to compare unfavourably with ours the performance of various sahibs he had climbed with, though he graciously conceded that Raymond Lambert went faster than we did! He ended up by telling us, with a grin of ill-concealed mischief, a few scandalous details about sahibs who had fallen by the wayside. I gleefully translated all this to Betty, who looked gratified but slightly taken aback. On the whole, Mingma's surprising outburst had a slightly tonic effect on us, which was no doubt what he had intended.

I now took over the lead from Ang Temba. By this time it was very steep, though the snow was better. We went up and up and I seemed to have been kicking steps all my life. Betty quite suddenly fell into a hidden crevasse, which Ang Temba and I had crossed in blissful ignorance. But she only went in up to her waist and quickly extricated herself. Contrary to her own belief, she was climbing steadily and well, and she certainly never once held us up as she seemed to think she was doing. In fact, the only indication we had of the effort she was making was her inability to reply to comments or questions. She literally did not have sufficient breath left to do so.

I went on kicking steps and gasping and stopping and going on again till we came to the ice. I cut steps up it, then up some frozen snow, then up more ice. When the snow became soft once more Ang Temba took over for a while until we had another rest, and then I went ahead again. The last stretch up to the col was all hard snow which only needed a couple of strokes with the axe, and this bit was fun. As we reached the col, across which a high wind was blowing drifting snow, I felt the excitement which had been mounting inside me all the way up reach a climax. Tibet lay below us, not all mountains this time as we had seen it from the lower col, but a great rolling brown plateau, with purple shadows, very restful to the eye after days and days of ice, snow and rock. We had hoped to see Gosanthan from here, but were disappointed. We think it was hidden from us by an isolated mountain massif which rose almost due north of where we stood. To our left the frontier ridge ran up as a rock shoulder leading to the magnificent peak north of Dorje Lakpa, which we called (with a certain poverty of imagination) the big white peak. Beyond lay the Lantang Himal. On our right were the shining slopes of pure ice leading to our dome. As usual the ridge fell away abruptly on the Tibetan side, and was overhung at the col by a terrific cornice which prevented us going too close to the edge.

We ate some mint cake, took photographs and put on our crampons. It was bitterly cold, and we needed our three pairs of gloves. We now noticed with dismay that the clouds were coming up fast from the south and were unusually black and menacing. If any of us were to reach the summit before it became enveloped in mist we should have to get a move on. It had already taken us three and a half hours to reach the col. So we untied and roped up again, Mingma and I on one rope and Betty and Ang Temba on the other.

Mingma and I set off up the ice, our crampons gripping well. I had hoped to lead all the way, because I felt fit and energetic, but the sight of those clouds made me abandon the idea in the interests of the expedition. If Mingma led in his present exalted mood, I should have to follow at his pace and we should get up much quicker than if I led at my own slower pace. This turned out to be a wise decision, though at times I thought I was going to die. Mingma went up that ice very nearly at a run with me tearing after him. We had never before moved so fast in the mountains, and I was now higher than I had ever been before—we must have been well over 21,000 feet. I could not get my breath fast enough at the pace at which we were climbing, and once stopped, gasping that I *must* halt. Mingma said anxiously, " The clouds, memsahib." They were very near and the sight of them spurred me on to greater efforts. Suddenly, Mingma stopped, and, with a beaming smile pointed and said, " Look, the summit." We saw the ice-slope easing off ahead to end suddenly in an unexpected little apex of snow. The sight of it was like a dose of oxygen. I took an enormous breath, said, " All right, come on," and we went up side by side to the summit.

Our mountain ended as if cut off by a chisel, and a big cornice overhung the Tibetan side. While Mingma fished out our little orange marking-flag, tied it to his ice-axe and stuck it in the snow, I looked round to see what I could of the mountains before they were swallowed up by a mass of cloud. There were the three peaks of Dorje Lakpa, easily recognisable but looking strangely small and far off. Close at hand was the beautiful shell-like fluting on the curved ridge of the big white peak. Then I caught sight of Phurbi Chyachu. Could we really be looking *down* on the plateau of her summit? I cried out, " Mingma, we're *higher* than Phurbi Chyachu," and he replied proudly, " Yes, higher, memsahib." This pleased us immensely, because, I suppose, this mountain loomed over us so intimidatingly at base camp. As if she objected to being seen at such an unbecoming angle, Phurbi Chyachu promptly veiled herself in cloud. The clouds had come up fast, but fortunately not quite so fast as we had.

After devoting a few rather painful minutes to photography, we sat down to drink water flavoured with lemon fizz and to talk companionably. Twenty minutes later we decided to go down and see what had happened to Betty and Ang Temba. We picked up all our gear, untied the flag from the axe and stuck its stick into the snow, and turned to leave. Suddenly we both stopped, struck by the same thought. There was something vital we had forgotten to do! There and then we shook hands with great éclat, comfortably aware that there were no witnesses to observe this display of conventionality. We began to descend, but before we had gone far were delighted to see Betty and Ang Temba coming up, only about half an hour behind us. A very good effort, for Betty's crampons had come adrift again and Ang Temba (for some mysterious Sherpa reason) had not brought any with him, so that they had to cut steps all the way up.

We went back to the summit to wait for them, and I sat down, feeling very smug and virtuous, and wrote out captions for the photographs I had taken. Unfortunately they turned out later to be more or less indecipherable. When the other two came up we shook hands all round for good measure. (The Sherpas entered into this with great zest, especially Ang Temba, to whom it was a new game) and we took a lot more photographs. Then we celebrated with mint cake and chocolate. We had no altimeter, but, judging from our position in relation to the known heights of Dorje Lakpa, Phurbi Chyachu, and the big white peak, we reckoned we were now at about 22,000 feet. Mingma insisted that we were higher, much higher, citing his symptoms once more. He said he had never before in all his experience had such difficulty in breathing. I assured him that people who try to run up Himalayan peaks must expect a little trouble of that sort. . . .

By this time, unusually dark clouds had covered most of the mountains, though the Tibetan plateau was still clear. The wind was rising too, and it had become very cold. I began to lose sensation in my hands and thought it was time to beat a retreat. Betty put her crampons on again, and, leaving the flag still stuck into the snow of the summit like an infinitesimal cherry on a colossal ice-cream, we began to descend as quickly as we could. As we did so we realised that these clouds heralded a real storm. The wind, growing stronger and colder all the time, fairly battered at us and when we reached the col we were set upon by whirling clouds of driven snow. Betty, conscientious to the last, stopped there to take compass bearings, but I had spent an hour of inactivity on the summit, and was very cold and wanted to keep going. So Mingma and I set off ahead, plunging down into the mist.

The descent seemed endless, but at last we reached the big snow-filled crevasse. I wanted to go round it this time, but Mingma was very much against this. He argued that a big storm was coming, that the weather was already very bad and that we had no time to waste. The snow had been perfectly firm before. It would still be safe. I was cold and tired and ready to believe him. Telling myself against my better judgment that I was light, and that Mingma was extremely strong, I agreed to cross the crevasse, but told Mingma to give me a good belay with his ice-axe until I reached the other side, where I would perform the same office for him. I set off across the doubtful snow, testing it at every step with my ice-axe and liking it less and less. Feeling the rope slacken, I turned round, and saw that Mingma had not waited but was following me. I was about to tell him to go back, but then decided that as I was only a few feet from the farther edge, it would be better for me to go on. I stepped forward, the snow gave way under me like an oubliette, and I fell through the crust. As I fell, I flung myself forward and drove the pick of my ice-axe into the snow-ice which formed the lip of the crevasse. Mingma tightened the rope at once, and held me, so that I fell no farther. I quickly wedged my right arm over the

176

corniced lip and found to my relief that the wall of the crevasse sloped towards me, so that I could gain purchase on it for one foot. Mingma shouted, " Thik hai, memsahib, I can pull you out," and I felt the tension of the rope around my waist increase. I did not at all want him to pull me out backwards. It would only break more of the crust and would probably result in our both being precipitated into the crevasse together. So I shouted to him to give me more rope, but my voice was muffled because I was under the snow and he did not hear me. The pain of the rope became almost intolerable, and I shouted again. This time he heard and the strain slackened. With my left hand I broke away enough of the brittle cornice to enable me to get the other arm out and to wriggle the rest of my body after it. Once safely on solid ice again I belayed Mingma as best I could while he crawled the rest of the way on his stomach. . . .

Thoroughly ashamed, and well aware that our party had no business to be on such a dangerous glacier roped in twos, we waited for Betty and Ang Temba to join us. Four chastened people then began to negotiate the traverse of the ice-slope on the other side. The skin of snow had melted away and the ice was now very slippery. We had taken off our crampons higher up because the snow was balling up under them, and, rather than replace them with half-frozen fingers, I began to cut steps all along the exposed stretch. Mingma, who did not seem to have profited by the fright he had just received, expostulated that this was unnecessary. But Betty supported me, and this time we were prepared to back our own judgment firmly. If one of us had slipped and fallen on that slope the whole party might well have slid helplessly into the crevasse below.

Once past this hazard we battled downwards through the icy gale and driving snow to the camp. It looked small and forlorn when we reached it, and showed no signs of life. However, our shouts brought an answer from Evelyn's tent, and good old Kusung came out of his, exclaimed at our appearance, and began pulling ineffectually at the ice which coated our balaclavas, gloves and socks. We were staggering with weariness by then, and, to be truthful, our one desire was to brush him off and get under cover. When we succeeded in doing so as politely as we could, and had crawled into our tents, Betty dropped down on her sleeping-bag still covered with snow. Evelyn was feeling very ill, but she got up and took off Betty's boots for her—a gesture of goodwill which was truly appreciated. I lost no time in stripping off frozen outer-layers of clothing and scrambled thankfully into the sleeping-bag I had so reluctantly quitted that morning. It had been an exciting and eventful day. We decided that we would probably feel pleased about the mountain next morning, but all that concerned us now was whether the Sherpas who remained in camp had had the gumption to melt snow for tea against our return. There are times when a mug of tea assumes an importance in a climber's life which is not to be underestimated.

CHAPTER THIRTEEN

The Storm

THE STORM gathered impetus during the night. Lightning flickered restlessly among the mountain tops, and the answering roll of thunder was almost drowned by the howling of the wind. But we were too tired to be disturbed by it and fell asleep as to a lullaby.

We woke in the morning to find the camp enveloped in grey storm-rack mingled with swirling eddies of powder snow swept up into the air by the tremendous wind. Directly we unzipped our tent doors to look out, an icy spray of fine snow blew in which coated everything inside with a most unwelcome film of glistening white. This was a true Himalayan storm, and we realised that it precluded all climbing that day. We mentally cancelled all engagements and sank back luxuriously into our sleeping-bags.

We lay all day reading, dozing and listening to the gusts of wind that drummed at the frail walls of our tents. The poor Sherpas in the Palomine had a bad time. It blew down once, and the lighted Primus burned a hole in it. They managed to erect it again, and luckily it had a fly-sheet which prevented the wind getting into the hole and ripping the tent apart.

Ang Temba struggled across to our tents three times with cocoa in the kettle and soup thickened with meat bar. We were indeed grateful to him. For the rest, we had dried fruit, sweets, chocolate, biscuits, and high altitude rations in our rucksacks, the consumption of which helped to pass the time as well as to preserve the unity of body and soul. For mental sustenance I had *The Confessions of Rousseau,* a work which alternately bored and infuriated me, but which I was resolved to finish. I found Rousseau a powerful soporific, an aspect of his writing not to be underrated at high altitudes where sleep is not always easy to come by.

At some time in the afternoon Betty put on every garment she possessed, including windproofs, and crawled across the few feet which separated her tent from mine to pay a social call. The two of us, comparing notes, found that our tongues and the inside of our mouths were very sore. After puzzling over this for some time and rejecting several unpleasant explanations, such as scurvy and trench-mouth, the truth dawned upon us. We had panted for air so constantly the previous day that *the insides of our mouths were sunburned!*

Contrary to our expectation, the wind did not die down that night, and once again we fell asleep to its dismal howling and the shuddering of the tent walls. We woke at dawn to see the glow of sunlight on the canvas, which encouraged us to think that we might be able to climb this morning to the col overlooking the Dorje Lakpa glacier, a somewhat optimistic assumption in view of the fact that the gale was stronger than ever. It came screaming through the funnel of the col and fell upon our camp as if it hated it. We unzipped our doors and peered out, to be covered at once with driven snow. The sky was temporarily clear overhead, but ugly cirrus stormclouds were hanging over the lower part of the glacier, and over the Tibetan mountains.

After a shouted colloquy the three of us agreed that as the sun was shining the storm *must* have abated somewhat. We all felt the need to retire out of sight down the glacier, and this slight lull was an opportunity not to be lost. Putting on our boots, all our sweaters, windproofs and two pairs of gloves, we went out. The cold struck us like a blow. It seemed strange and almost sinister to see the sunshine reflected brilliantly from the snow surface, polished smooth by the wind, and to find no warmth in it at all, no tempering of the cruel wind. Going down the glacier was bad enough, but battling our way up the slope against the wind, half-blinded by powder snow blown into our smarting faces, we began to wonder seriously if we ever would regain the tents. It was an experience none of us is likely to forget.

I was away longer than the others, and by the time I reached my tent my right hand had lost all sensation and was useless. The zip on my tent door was very stiff (a zip-opening to a mountain tent is never a good idea) and I struggled to open it with my left hand for what seemed an age. It yielded at last, but my left hand was now going the way of the right and I could not close the zip again. Meantime gusts of wind blew more and more snow into the tent. At last I got the door closed and sat there, breathless, covered from head to foot with a film of snow, like everything else in the tent. Then my hands began to come back to life, and I rolled over on my sleeping-bag in agony. The pain was so great that I thought I was going to be sick. However, it passed off after a bit and I began to feel better.

Later, at about eight o'clock, Mingma made a dash for our tents and announced that there was not much food left. He thought we ought to go down while the going was good. We thought so too, though we sorely regretted having to leave that western col unvisited. It was decided that we should wait until nine o'clock before breaking camp, in the hope that there might be more warmth in the sun by then.

At nine, we once more put on our windproofs over all our layers of clothing, pulling the hoods well forward to protect as much of our faces as possible. Sherpas and memsahibs alike plunged with one accord into a hectic scramble to pack away gear and take the tents down before the cold rendered us incapable of movement. It was no easy task. The guys and pegs were frozen into the snow, the poles were frozen together. We dug furiously with our ice-axes to find and release the buried pegs and bundled the tents together anyhow, one after another, poles sticking out in all directions. Before we had finished, the clouds were upon us, blotting out everything except ourselves, a little group of labouring figures in a grey and hostile world of wind, mist and intense cold.

Mingma urged me to lead off with the other memsahibs and the slower Sherpas, while he and Ang Temba took down the last tent. This I was very glad to do as I could no longer feel my hands and feet. Using the longest rope, we set off down the glacier, trying to follow the footprints we had made coming up. But this was not easy. Drifting snow had filled, and in places entirely obliterated, our tracks, and the impossibility of seeing more than a few yards ahead in the mist made it hard to pick them up again once lost. The pace at which we started was of my choosing, for my instinctive reaction was to get down out of the terrible wind before the blood congealed in my veins. But three days of starvation and altitude sickness had so weakened Evelyn that she was incapable of going fast. The same applied to Kusung. Betty had to keep shouting, " Slower, please; they want you to go slower."

It is interesting to note here that though it was an advantage to me, while actually climbing, to be so thin and slight, I felt the cold more than either of my companions. Evelyn (possibly because, though we were all fairly lean, she was the best-covered of the three) felt it least of all. Even during the storm at Camp V, when she was really unwell, she only wore a string vest and a pair of cotton pants inside her sleeping-bag. Betty felt the cold more than Evelyn but nothing like as much as I did. It seems, therefore, that it might be a good idea to put *on* weight, if possible, before going on a Himalayan expedition.

Just before we reached the séracs we were joined by Mingma and Ang Temba. After casting about we found our tracks once more and followed them to the knife-edge bridge across the highest crevasse. I started to lead across this. The old steps along the top had been filled up and I had to make new ones. All went well until I was about two-thirds of the way across, and Betty, following me, was also embarked on the crossing. Then, to everyone's alarm, including my own, I stopped, swayed dangerously, and said, " Sorry, I can't see. My glasses have misted up." Snow goggles are generally strapped round the head with a broad adjustable elastic band. This band had slipped down, pulling the glasses tight against my eyes and completely blurring my vision. It was not possible in my precarious position to put this right, because the hood of my *anorak* was zipped and laced up and I was wearing windproof fingerless mittens over two pairs of gloves. The knife-edge was all right if one kept moving along it, but it was no place on which to stand about. For one thing there was no room to place both feet together on it. I started to move on slowly, standing on one foot while feeling blindly for the next step with the other. Betty watched me, waiting to see which way I would fall, and ready to throw herself into the crevasse on the other side, which would be the only way of holding me. Fortunately, it was not necessary to do this, though there was one bad moment just as I asked, " Am I across? " Betty replied, " Yes, but keep to the right." Whereupon I stepped half-wittedly to the left and almost walked into the crevasse after all. A concerted yell of warning went up from the enthralled onlookers and disaster was averted.

The bridge across the debris in the great crevasse, about which we had all been a little anxious, went surprisingly well. But once on the other side of it we lost our old tracks completely. The mist was thicker than ever when it was down, but we noticed that it kept rising sufficiently for us to get glimpses of the snow corridor, separated from where we were by a section of the ice-fall which looked rather like a white sponge, so full was it of crevasses running irregularly in all directions. We began to pick our way cautiously across it in the direction of the corridor.

Our progress was slow. The mist and the crevasses prevented our taking a straight line; Evelyn, suffering from nausea, had to keep stopping to be sick; and Kusung seemed very weak. He slipped and fell once, as we were negotiating the descent from a sérac, and, though Betty held him with a turn of the rope round her ice-axe, which she drove hard into the snow, he dropped his load. It rolled down and fell out of sight. We were shattered by this catastrophe, because Kusung was carrying the sleeping-bags and air-mattresses. It could be a serious matter if these were lost. Our relief may be imagined when we reached the foot of the slope and turned a corner to see the load lying safely at the very edge of a crevasse.

Crossing the " sponge " led us a strange dance, in thick mist, in and out and around the crevasses. The mist rose for a moment and enabled us to take a bearing on the site of Camp IV. Then it came down again, and we groped our way forward with crevasses looming up right and left.

At last, to our relief, we found ourselves in the corridor. At Camp IV we picked up a box containing some spare gear, and here we untied and rearranged the ropes; Mingma, Ang Temba, Bahu and I on one rope to go on ahead and route-find, Betty, Evelyn, Chhepala and Kusung to follow on the other. But as it turned out, route-finding was unnecessary. The line of steps we had made on our way up led, always just visible as a faint trace in the snow, up and down the obstacles on the ice-fall. Besides this, we found ourselves descending below the level of the clouds and were once more able to see down to the main glacier. The sky was still dark and stormy, but the storm was clearly receding, and we were not even subjected to the usual afternoon snowfall.

Having made sure that Betty's rope was also off the ice-fall, our party went away, almost at a trot, down the main glacier towards the two big boulders of Camp IIA. As we approached the eastern side of the glacier, we saw that the snow was covered with great blocks of ice which had fallen from the hanging glaciers of Phurbi Chyachu. A big thaw had evidently taken place lower down, while the storm raged at Camp V. We reached Camp IIA, where, incidentally, we had left a box containing some extra food, and began to put up the tents. The others arrived about half an hour later, Evelyn going much faster now and looking a better colour already. We all rejoiced in the comparative warmth and comfort of being about two thousand five hundred feet lower in altitude, and out of the cruel wind. That night Evelyn had her first real meal for days.

The storm had let us off lightly. Both Evelyn and I had our toes slightly touched by frostbite, which gave us a certain amount of pain for a few days. But this soon wore off. Two or three of Evelyn's toenails were blackened, and I lost a nail and could not feel the tips of my toes for a few weeks. Betty and the Sherpas were quite unscathed by the cold. We considered ourselves very lucky.

In the morning all signs of the storm clouds had vanished, though every mountain still flew a windsock of blown snow. We could see that the gale still swept the site of Camp V and were very glad to be out of it. We had tentatively planned to make one last sortie up the glacier, to visit the low col above the ice-fall at its head, which we thought might possibly be a pass (albeit a difficult and dangerous one) into Tibet. But when I went over to the kitchen tent to discuss this project with Mingma, I found the Sherpas plunged in gloom. In spite of repeated warnings Ang Temba and Bahu had removed their dark glasses to see better in the mist the day before, with the result that they were now both snowblind. With Kusung they lay in their tents, refusing food. Chhepala was well but seemed to have fallen under the influence of the pervading atmosphere of pessimism. Mingma was quite fit, but he too was unhappy. His boots were falling apart and he had left his spare pair at base camp. Also the food that remained to us was not of the sort to appease a hungry Sherpa's appetite. All the Sherpas wanted to do was to go home to base camp— Mingma as much as any of them. He did not admit to this, of course, but pointed out the food shortage and said that the other Sherpas had had enough hardship for the present. In the end, we had to give in and agree to the whole party going back together. It was just as well we did so, as it turned out.

We packed up, not so fast as usual because Ang Temba and Bahu were sitting sadly about on food boxes clasping their smarting eyes, and then we set off slowly down the glacier guiding the two blind lads. We noticed at once that the thaw caused by the strengthening of the moonsoon current had progressed steadily over the past week. The glacier was now comparatively clear of snow, but this did not improve matters. The bigger crevasses were, it is true, more evident, as their snow covering had sunk a little, revealing their shape. But in the case of the smaller crevasses the top covering of frozen snow still disguised them, while the snow underneath had melted. The first intimation we had of this was when Betty fell without warning through the crust into a crevasse over which four of us had already walked. Fortunately, (as she was leading the second rope, followed by the blind Ang Temba, who was not in a position to safeguard her) she threw herself backward when she felt the snow collapse and her rucksack caught on the edge and held her. Ang Temba and Chhepala managed to pull her out without much trouble, but it was this incident which first drew our attention to the extent to which the glacier had changed in character.

It was, however, not until we reached the top of the ice-fall that this fact was truly brought home to us. The ice-fall was no longer a familiar friend but a potential enemy. It was especially dangerous near the top. Where all had been firm snow before was now a wilderness of twisting crevasses covered with a layer of rotten snow. Once embarked on this sinister passage we began to sweat freely. We would jump crevasses to find the surface upon which we landed beginning to disintegrate under our feet. We would plunge our ice-axes in to give a belay to the next on the rope, only to feel the ice-axe go through into empty air. There did not seem to be a moment when one or several of us was not conscious of being perched on a tenuous crust of melting snow over yet another apparently bottomless well. To make matters worse each rope was handicapped by the presence of a blind man who had to be shepherded across the obstacles. Perhaps the only one of us who remained comparatively unperturbed by our situation was Bahu, who had been so nervous on the way up this same ice-fall. He could not see the dangers now. It was probably just as well that he was blind this time, otherwise we might have had even more difficulty in getting him down.

Our steps had gone, and crumbling walls of rotten ice

confronted us where they had been. Comfortable snow-capped bridges had become unsafe knife-edges. Séracs had fallen, and the beautiful fringes of icicles had all vanished. The melting of the snow had revealed a mass of unattractive rubble clinging like fungus to the pock-marked ice. The whole face of the ice-fall had altered, and was now ugly and menacing. Still, we managed, by dint of lowering the loads separately and cutting a great many steps of varying reliability, to avert one minor crisis after another.

There was a particular hazard about which we speculated quite a lot as we approached it. This was a big crevasse which we had hitherto crossed by an ice-bridge on which we had never cared to linger, as its look of fragility had not inspired us with much confidence. We were certain that the bridge would no longer be in existence, and we were right. When we reached the crevasse there was no sign of it. But Mingma, though muttering at intervals, " I don't like it," was equal to this emergency. While Evelyn and I were considering a different escape route altogether, which would have meant cutting endless steps and eventually running the gauntlet of falling rock and ice, Mingma pounced on a solution, which was certainly far quicker, though whether it was also safer is debatable. This involved making a descent into the crevasse, crossing it by a tired-looking hump of snow which still blocked it at that point, and cutting a ladder of steps up the opposite wall of the crevasse. This route, though a trifle hair-raising, proved to be adequate, in spite of the fact that the soundness of the snow-ice up which Mingma cut his steps left much to be desired.

Once across this crevasse the remainder of the ice-fall went fairly well, though it had to be taken slowly. But at last both parties were safely down and scrambling along the narrow and boulder-strewn snow corridor which led to the site of Camp I. This corridor was a chute for falling rocks and lumps of ice. Mingma, who was more afraid of stone-fall than of anything else, urged us, almost tearfully, to hurry. Once we had all foregathered safely at the site of Camp I he spoke his mind. " Memsahib," he said firmly, " the ice-fall is finished till after the monsoon. I, for one, am not going up there again. It is very dangerous." We were in complete agreement. Pass or no pass, there was going to be no competition among our number to try any more conclusions with that ice-fall in its new guise.

While we were eating jam with snow and exclaiming at the changes wrought by the thaw, we heard a distant shout and saw a black speck moving across the snow between us and base camp. It was Lakpa, the Tempathang Sherpa boy, who had been keeping a lookout for us the last day or two from the boulder-covered spur between base camp and the snow slopes. Now he was making his way towards us, using a stick as an ice-axe, to lend a hand with the loads. We were all pleased to see his cheerful face, and Ang Temba and Bahu, whose sight was returning, were even able to exchange grins with him.

The last long trudge back was not as bad as usual. True, the gullies were as untrustworthy as ever and the snow so soft that we sank into it thigh-deep, but once over the boulder-covered spur we found ourselves in a new world. The snow had all gone, revealing the grass and juniper it had covered, from which the sun drew a scent which filled our nostrils with sweetness. There was no afternoon snow-fall this day. The sun shone, flowers were everywhere, and birds sang. We had walked straight out of winter into summer, and we repressed with difficulty a desire to throw ourselves down and embrace the warm living earth which received us back so kindly.

CHAPTER FOURTEEN

Home from the Hill

THIS TIME base camp really was the haven we had pictured. We arrived there strolling along with jerseys stuffed into our rucksacks, shirt-sleeves rolled up, flowers tucked into our caps, and carrying bunches of cowslips at which we sniffed like Ferdinand. Murari, Ang Droma and Nima Lama greeted us like returning prodigals—indeed so affectionately that we suspected that they had become somewhat bored with each other's company in our absence.

We sank down on the warm dry grass and asked for water, lots and lots of water. We were told that Mingma (who had hurried ahead, as a good sirdar should, to lay on nourishment) had prepared soup for us. Soup? Soup was salty. We wanted water, in which to put orange juice or lemon fizz. This message was conveyed to Mingma, who sent back a firm reply. We could not have anything but soup, because Kusung had not arrived yet and he was carrying the mugs. But Mingma had our plates and he was giving us soup because that was the only liquid one could legitimately drink out of plates. The implication was that if we wanted water we could go and drink it out of the burn. Mingma was not going to subscribe to any flouting of convention, and it was clear that in his opinion people who wished to drink orange juice out of the wrong kind of container were pretty common.

So we had soup. Then we had hot potatoes baked in the embers of the kitchen fire. When Kusung turned up we had orange juice and lemon fizz. After that we had tea, more potatoes, biscuits and jam, and sardines. These snacks served as an apéritif for the serious business of supper, which was ready at about six.

We generally ate much more at base camp than anywhere else, because with time on his hands Mingma would think up special treats for us, and we were always being given elevenses and " fly-cuppies." Higher up, of course, the afternoon was eating-time. Nobody felt very hungry at six o'clock in the morning, and the only solid food we could ever manage to get down at halts while climbing was chocolate, mint cake, dried fruit or boiled sweets. But once settled in our tents we would have things to eat and drink every hour or so until we fell asleep.

In the evening Mingma threw armfuls of wood on the kitchen fire. The sweet scent of burning juniper proved irresistible. We gathered round the splendid blaze and had our supper there. One by one the Sherpas joined us, with the exception of Ang Temba and Bahu, who had retired to sleep off their snow-blindness. It was a memorable meal. We had rice mixed with " *masala* " (curry spices) and *dhal*, and a kind of green vegetable which Nima Lama had brought up with him. It was the sort we had found growing at Pemsal on our way up from Tempathang. We discovered in ourselves a craving for fresh green food, and this weed tasted better to us than early asparagus or new peas.

Phurbi Chyachu and all the other peaks retained the afterglow of sunset until it was almost dark, and we gazed at them dreamily through the wood-smoke, asking the Tempathang men their own names for the peaks and glaciers, ridges and valleys. It occurred to us that the lower southward-running ridge of the Phurbi Chyachu chain, which faced us across the valley of the Pulmutang Khola, looked very beguiling. There were two charming little alps about half-way up which lay below the rapidly receding snowline, and which looked to be perfect camp-sites. South of a small peak of about nineteen thousand odd feet, which had an unmistakeable ice-cap, the Sherpas told us that the snow completely disappeared from this ridge in the monsoon, and the slopes below the rocky crest were suitable grazing grounds for yaks and goats. In some places it was even possible, they said, to cross over to the Nosem Khola, whose valley lay on the far side of the ridge. They added a rider to the effect that the bed of one of the hanging glaciers just south of the summit of Phurbi Chyachu would make a splendid pass over the frontier ridge, and that the yak-herds of Tempathang were waiting for the glacier to recede out of existence so that they could start using it. This was taking the long-term view with a vengeance, and we could not ourselves work up much enthusiasm over a state of affairs unlikely to come about in our lifetime. But we thought we would like to find out something about the lower passes and also to look at the upper reaches of the Nosem Khola, and the small glaciers beyond it. We came to the conclusion that one of us should make this trip while the others crossed over to the Dorje Lakpa glacier. Evelyn was particularly attracted to the ridge, which looked as if it would provide delightful climbing at more comfortable altitudes than those at which we had been travelling recently, while Betty was extremely keen to find approaches to the Dorje Lakpa glacier, and the smaller ones farther west. We knew these were inaccessible from below.

When it became quite dark, Betty and Evelyn decided to call it a day and retire to their tents. I sat on with the Sherpas and Murari, discussing names for the mountains and glaciers we had discovered. We had already told Mingma that we wanted to call the mountain we had climbed after him, as a tribute to his enthusiasm and enterprise. He was very pleased and rather overcome, but expressed a wish, for some reason we could not fathom, that it should be called after his second name rather than his first. We were quite agreeable, and the only thing that bothered us was that there seemed to be no word in the Sherpa " *boli* " for dome. " Gyalgen Tsucho "—(Gyalgen Peak) sounded fine, but we could not help thinking that the word peak was not entirely appropriate when applied to the rounded summit of our mountain. The glacier which led to it was easier to name. We did feel that it would be nice to leave some reminder for posterity of our pioneering, so it was christened " The Ladies' Glacier." We also annexed to ourselves the high col, calling it " The Ladies' Col." To the lower col we reached on the frontier ridge, where we had built the chorten, we gave a gaelic name—" The Bealach." The Sherpas and I also discussed several names for the twenty-three thousander, which, incidentally, we had no right to christen, as convention demands that one must be the first to climb a nameless mountain before taking it upon oneself to name it. However, the debate came to an abrupt end when Murari said reverently, " The Sherpas think the mountain should be called " The Big White Peak." This is a very beautiful English name." At this I started to giggle, thereby greatly mystifying poor Murari, and had to agree hastily that nothing could be more suitable. So that is how the big white peak became known officially to the expedition as The Big White Peak.

In the morning we all slept fairly late, though Evelyn outdid all of us by several hours. So much so that around eleven o'clock, when there was still no sign of life from her tent, the Sherpas began to make anxious inquiries after her health. On being told that she was merely rebuilding her tissues—or words to that effect—they cheered up and cast about to find something to do which would please us. They hit upon the right idea when they erected the fly-sheet of the Palomine once again as a screen, and set up the canvas bath on four ice-axes. This was very well received indeed, and the memsahibs made full use of the bathroom, getting through many cans of hot water and having a field day laundering their smalls.

We always hung our brassières and pants out to dry as modestly as possible, generally on the guys at the back of our tents. But to no avail. Kusung or Chhepala would invariably come along later, cluck disapprovingly, as if to say, " These will *never* dry here," and cart them off to the public drying-lines, where they would thereafter blow in the breeze among rows of Sherpa underwear. On one occasion, when Evelyn had washed her underclothes and hung them up in a secluded place, it began to rain. Everyone dashed about dragging things under cover, and just as the whole party was making for shelter a shout was heard from Chhepala. He came towards the camp waving Evelyn's smalls and roundly ticking off Ang Droma for forgetting about them! The truth is that while our Sherpas were as sensitive and delicate as possible over things that mattered, they had no false modesty, and it thus never occurred to them to be the slightest bit coy about feminine underwear. This sensible attitude was a great relief to us.

While we bathed ourselves, Chhepala and Kusung put up the drying-lines, and Ang Droma scrubbed away in her laundry, using, as usual, immense quantities of soap. Murari, Mingma, Ang Temba and Bahu wandered about picking flowers. They had seen us coming in with bunches of them the day before, and had obviously come to the conclusion that a bit of Constance Spry would be appreciated by us. An empty jam-jar was commandeered as a vase, into which as many flowers were crammed as possible. The colourful but rapidly wilting result was then proudly placed in the middle of the medical box, which we used as our dining-table at base camp.

The day passed peacefully. Evelyn woke and repaired to the bath, while Betty and I went up to the lochan to test an air-mattress for leaks. We soon got side-tracked, and spent the afternoon very pleasantly " bouldering " barefoot. The clouds came up at the usual time but dispersed later, and when it became cold we all gravitated to the fire once more. This time the Tempathang Sherpas entertained us with songs and dances. Their tunes and rhythms reminded us very much of Highland songs and pipe music, while their dances bore a resemblance to Scottish country dancing, though they were rather less energetic. One of the little songs they sang began proudly, " Our Tenzing has climbed Everest."

It had been decided that Evelyn should go down to Pemsal the following day, cross the Pulmutang and climb up the opposite ridge, called by the Tempathang Sherpas the Chaksil Danda. From her highest camp she would find a way to the crest of the Chaksil Danda ridge and take photographs and bearings of the Nosem Khola valley, its glaciers, if possible, and the peaks beyond. She would have Chhepala and Ang Temba with her. As this party would not be returning to Pomba Serebu, and as the other party would only return to pack up for a final departure, we decided that Murari, Ang Droma and Lakpa would accompany Evelyn as well—Murari as interpreter and Ang Droma and Lakpa as porters. Nima Lama was to go down to Tempathang and bring or send up fourteen volunteers from there to carry for us back to Kathmandu. Meanwhile, Betty and I with Mingma, Kusung and Bahu, would climb to the pass we had discovered above base camp, and find a way down to the Dorje Lakpa glacier, which the Tempathang people called the Nyakarkarbu. We would cross the glacier, if possible, and make a camp on the far side. During the next two days we would try to climb to the crest of the south ridge of Dorje Lakpa, the lower slopes of which looked easy and the upper part extremely uninviting. From the top we hoped to take bearings and photograph the peaks and glaciers to the west of Dorje Lakpa, which were drained by the Langtang Khola, another tributary of the Balephi.

In the late afternoon a man and a woman turned up with presents of eggs and *rakhsi*, the local spirit. They hailed from Tempathang, and had walked for three days and made the steep and long ascent from Pemsal in the hope of receiving treatment from Evelyn for the woman's eyes. Unfortunately for the poor soul there was not much that could be done for her. Her eyes were scarred by ulcers due to venereal disease, which had permanently impaired her sight. Evelyn put drops in them to help the inflammation and treated her husband for a cough.

The *rakhsi* was brought to us with great ceremony by our Sherpas, who expected us to be overjoyed. But, sad to say, the foreign memsahibs, who up to now had managed to compare fairly favourably in Sherpa eyes with foreign sahibs, turned out to have feet of clay after all. We tasted the *rakhsi* and found it revolting. With the best will in the world we could not swallow more than a few sips of the stuff, which was exceedingly strong and had a foul taste like rotting vegetation. Shaking their heads in concern (but probably saying to themselves, " All the more for us,") the Sherpas carried it away again to their own tent, while we hurried to the burn to rinse out our mouths.

That night we all foregathered round the fire again, our

visitors as well, to talk and to watch Nima Lama and Lakpa dance. Lakpa also played Sherpa melodies on his mouth-organ, a souvenir of a trading trip to Kathmandu, upon which he was no mean performer. It was all very friendly and happy. But as the evening went on we realised that the Sherpas were waiting politely for us to go to bed so as to get down to the *rakhsi* in a big way. We took the hint and wishing them good night went to our tents. The party became extremely noisy later, and went on till long past midnight. We woke up once or twice to hear our friends in full carousal, and wondered rather grimly how they would feel in the morning. Then we turned over and went determinedly to sleep again.

CHAPTER FIFTEEN

East and West

W^{E HAD} planned to rise at 5.30 a.m., pack up, and
leave camp by 8 a.m. At the appointed time,
therefore, the three memsahibs grumpily dragged themselves from their sleeping-bags and began to dress, but
nothing else happened for a long time. Eventually Bahu
and Ang Droma came stumbling out, he to pick up the
big water-carrying tin and take it to the burn, she to light
the cooking fire. Their elders continued to nurse their
hangovers under cover for about half an hour before they
began to appear, in ones and twos, looking wan and haggard.
We found ourselves stepping back smartly every time one
of them spoke to us, to avoid the *rakhsi* fumes that were
breathed liberally over us.

It was a disappointing morning, cold and cloudy. Betty
and I were very keen to get off as soon as possible because
we thought we might have some difficulty in finding our
way down to the Dorje Lakpa glacier from our pass. We
began pointedly to take down our tent, at the same time
inquiring when breakfast would be ready. Breakfast was
slow in coming, but when it came it was a notable meal
clearly designed to keep us quiet for a bit. It consisted of
two fried eggs each, fresh eggs such as we had not eaten
for weeks, accompanied by a large ladleful of boiled bamboo
shoots, which are delicious by any standard. We did

complete justice to this treat, and began to feel much more indulgent towards the dilatory but obviously penitent Sherpas.

But as the morning wore on our patience wore thin again. The packing up of gear was carried out with a painful slowness, and the Sherpas kept disappearing, probably to catch themselves a quick one. We had believed, erroneously it appeared, that the *rakhsi* was finished, and were slightly irritated to find it very much with us. Eventually Betty and I decided to start without them, and I said to Mingma rather shortly, " We're tired of waiting, so we're going on." He looked somewhat taken aback at this, but we hardened our hearts and picked up our rucksacks. We said good-bye to Evelyn and her party and, wishing them luck, set off together up the steep slopes towards the pass.

There was far less snow this time and it was in much better condition. The rocks on the crest of the ridge were almost free of snow and ice, and we had a pleasant scramble to the top. There we relented and stopped to wait for the Sherpas, to give them a hand with their loads up the rocks. They were some time coming and we got very chilly waiting, because the mountains were now in thick mist and it had started to snow. We could not even *see* the Dorje Lakpa glacier. The result was that by the time the Sherpas did arrive and everyone was safely up on the crest of the ridge, we were in no mood for social dalliance and moved off as fast as possible.

As we descended we began to catch glimpses of the glacier through gaps in the cloud, and saw with misgiving that on our side of it the snow slopes ended in steep cliffs of smooth rock which plunged vertically down to the ice. We began to think that we might have to camp on the near side of the glacier that night and not risk an attempt to climb down to it until the morning, when the weather would be clear. But just as we were debating this we reached a gully which looked as if it might descend right down to the glacier, though we could not be certain because of the thick mist. It seemed to lie at a comparatively easy angle, and as we crossed it Betty and I wondered aloud if it might prove a good route down. Of course, there was no way of telling what it did once out of sight. For all we knew it might plunge over the cliffs or peter out altogether. When we had crossed we climbed carefully downward along its farther rim, hoping to be able to see over the precipice. Mingma protested, saying that the gully would certainly not " go." Just then the clouds lifted for a moment and we saw all the way down to the glacier. We were right, the gully *would* " go." Mingma shook his head gloomily. It was much too dangerous, he said, his tone implying that anyone who wished to go down there was mad. It was not the angle he objected to, but the fact that the gully was littered with rocks which had fallen from its horribly friable walls. We agreed that this detracted from the gully's charm, but had Mingma any alternative to offer? He had not. Farther on, the cliffs became quite impossible, and it looked as if it were the gully or nothing. Betty and I were delighted, and while the Sherpas still hesitated, we climbed down into it, taking great care to avoid loosening stones, and began to descend. To our relief we found the snow excellent—so good in fact that we were able to enjoy our first glissade in the Himalaya. Seeing this, the Sherpas began to climb down after us, and a shower of large stones immediately thudded into the gully and whizzed past us like cannon balls. We stopped and yelled back at them to desist until we were safely down. Then we went on, slightly ill-at-ease now, until the gully ended on the stony moraine. We crossed this and went right on to the glacier to be out of

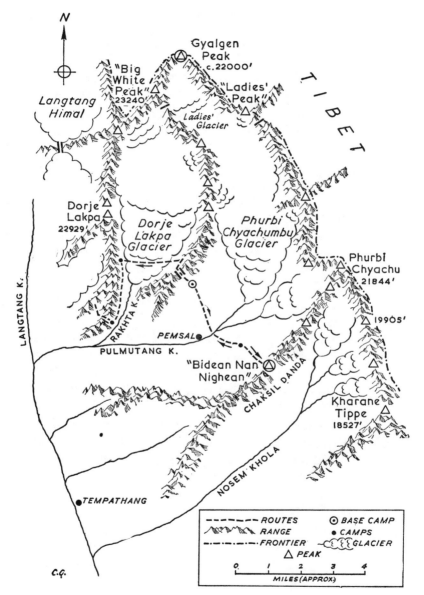

N

Gyalgen Peak
c.22000'

"Big White Peak" 23240'

Langtang Himal

"Ladies' Peak"

Ladies' Glacier

TIBET

Dorje Lakpa 22929'

Dorje Lakpa Glacier

Phurbi Chyachumbu Glacier

Phurbi Chyachu 21844'

19905'

LANGTANG K.

RAKHTA K.

PEMSAL

PULMUTANG K.

"Bidean Nan Nighean"

CHAKSIL DANDA

Kharane Tippe 18527'

NOSEM KHOLA

TEMPATHANG

C.G.

ROUTES   ⊙ BASE CAMP
RANGE   • CAMPS
FRONTIER   GLACIER
△ PEAK

0   1   2   3   4

MILES (APPROX)

reach of stonefall, and then signalled to the Sherpas to come on.

This level part of the Nyakarkar glacier was completely different from our Phurbi Chyachumbu. It was clear of snow, so that all the crevasses could easily be seen, and the ice was a dirty grey. It was littered with stones, and its western side was covered with piled-up boulders. It reminded me somewhat of the great Zemu glacier in the Sikkim Himalaya, and when Mingma arrived I remarked on this to him. He replied huffily that he did not agree. The Zemu was much bigger. Since this was unarguable I did not contradict him, but hoped that he would begin to feel better tempered soon.

We crossed the glacier quite easily. This was the only safe part of it; a level stretch between the rotten and dangerous upper ice-fall, which comprised at least two-thirds of the whole glacier, and the lower ice-fall above the nose, which ended in the gorge of the Rakhta Khola.

The moraine looked to be very insecure so we decided to camp among the boulders on the ice of the glacier itself, out of reach of stone-fall. There was no point in going higher, as visibility, except when the mist rose momentarily, was limited to a few yards, and we had no idea what lay beyond.

The weather cleared a little in the evening and Betty and I went out to watch the sun turn the clouds hiding Dorje Lakpa to pink and gold, and to do a bit of scrambling among the boulders. We liked this camp, uncomfortable though it had appeared to be at first sight. It struck us as a mysterious and exciting place and we found ourselves wanting to talk in whispers. As we were going back to our tent, we heard yet another roar, and saw two huge blocks of ice, as big as houses, peel slowly off the ice-fall and crash down, bursting into pieces and sending up clouds of splintered ice like spray. It was just too far off to menace us, but near enough to be tremendously impressive. We looked at each other. If there had been any question previously as to whether or not we should go up *that* ice-fall, there was none now.

We went back to our tent and climbed into our sleeping-bags, missing the cheerful songs and laughter we were wont to overhear from the Sherpas' tent. This evening all was silent. A deep depression, compounded of hangover, bad conscience and hurt pride brooded over them and communicated itself to us. For the first time Mingma did not come to say good night.

We woke to find the weather clear as we had hoped, and saw a sight that sent us reaching for our cameras. Immediately above us, springing up directly from the glacier, soared the three magnificent spires of Dorje Lakpa. They sparkled in the sun, steep and uncompromising. Dorje Lakpa is an incredible peak, straight out of an early Victorian artist's nightmare. It looks quite unclimbable.

That same sun which shone so brightly on the upper story of the mountain showed no signs of penetrating to the basement of the glacier for some while to come. Meanwhile it was chilly in the blue shadows. Nevertheless we had eaten breakfast by six and were impatient to be off. Just as we were rolling up the sleeping-bags, who should emerge from the Sherpa tent but Mingma himself, grinning from ear to ear, and bearing two beakers of splendid hot tea. That this bonus was an olive branch we had no doubt. Mingma's whole attitude showed that he intended to do all in his power to make amends. Indeed, his manner combined the solicitous with the affable to such an extent that it caused us to suspect, ungratefully, that he was primed with a hair of the dog that bit him. No sooner had we knocked back the tea than he appeared again with some more, bringing with him as well, to our great astonishment, a lighted Primus. This he placed on the ice between us, remarking that it was a cold morning and we would be well advised to warm our hands. It *was* cold, but no colder than a good many other mornings on this expedition, when nobody had suggested that we should warm our hands at anything. However, suppressing our mirth, we thawed out our hands at the flame. Mingma now dashed off busily, only to return carrying a steaming pan, the contents of which showed that we had been justified in our suspicions. The pan contained a plentiful supply of hot *rakhsi*, which he insisted we should take to warm us up. It would have been churlish to refuse, so we accepted it with a good grace. Betty drank hers neat, and I rather unwillingly laced my second cup of tea with it. It certainly did warm our stomachs temporarily, but it made us feel slightly sick for the rest of the morning.

Cheered by this interlude and by the reconciliation it symbolised, we all packed up camp, and after some argument as to the best route, climbed an ice-wall and scrambled up the moraine—quite a scramble, as it was disgustingly loose. Above the moraine we climbed gentle snowfields until after a couple of hours we reached a kind of vast shelf that lay above the precipices which fell to the gorge and below the rock crests of the south ridge of Dorje Lakpa. This was a fascinating place. Dotted with huge boulders and criss-crossed with the footprints of mountain sheep and marmots, it reminded me, somehow, of the lunar landscapes described in the science fiction of my childhood.

Betty and I now decided to ascend a small spur thrust out from the main mass of Dorje Lakpa, so as to take some photographs of the upper part of the glacier. The Sherpas wanted to come too, so we all deposited our loads and set off fast (so as to beat the inevitable clouds) up a steep incline, making for a col at the top of the spur.

When we reached it we saw that the col we had wanted to visit but had not reached from Camp V was indeed a true pass between the Ladies' Glacier and the Nyakarkarbu, the Dorje Lakpa glacier. The glacier itself looked worse than ever from this viewpoint. To get to the head of it or to climb The Big White Peak, it would be far better to ascend the Phurbi Chyachumbu and the Ladies' Glacier, and go over the pass. The pass itself is so high that a party taking that route would find themselves debouching on to the snowfields of The Big White Peak itself more than a quarter of the way up the south face of the mountain.

The mounting sea of cloud at last put an end to the photography session, and we descended quickly. First we glissaded down with wild yells, and then, reaching a steep grass slope, Kusung began to run. We all followed, hooting and shouting and racing each other, full of exhilaration born of good climbing, good health and good company. At the bottom we picked up our loads and went on until we found a beautiful camp-site on a flat snow-covered alp. As it had now started to snow hard, we put up the tents with all speed and scuttled into them for shelter.

Because the sun had been so slow in reaching the glacier we had finally lost patience and packed up the tents before the condensation of the night had quite evaporated. Betty and I now had cause to regret our haste. The snowfall of the afternoon was heavy and wet, and it began to come through the damp roof of our tent, oozing in furtively at first, but rapidly turning into an indoor rainstorm. We bore it as long as we could, covering the sleeping-bags with *anoraks* and windproof trousers, but it soon became clear that such temporary makeshifts were not sufficient. There was a large rambler's rain cape in one of the kitbags and when Bahu appeared with soup we asked him to spread it over the top of our tent. Though willing, Bahu was not as bright as he might have been, and he spread the cape in such a way that, while one side of our tent was protected, the other leaked worse than ever. Since mine was the wet side it fell to me to put on my boots and crawl out into the snow to put the cape on straight. While I was struggling with it I heard a smothered giggle, and turning round, saw three grinning faces peering out of the Sherpa tent. Our situation was of the sort which appeals strongly to the Sherpa sense of humour, and by their delighted expressions I gathered that their tent was considerably dryer inside than ours. I waved to them in what I hoped was the manner of one who snaps her fingers at hardship and crawled in again. As a matter of fact we slept quite peacefully that night. It was warm, and by the morning everything in the tent had dried out quite well.

At 7.30 a.m., Betty, Mingma and I set off as hard as we could in the hope of getting to the crest of the Dorje Lakpa south ridge before the clouds came up. The climbing was varied and interesting and we came to the conclusion that this part of the Jugal Himal was an enchanting place, full of surprises. We wished we had more time in which to do it justice by exploring it thoroughly.

A long gully and a last snow shoulder led us to the top of the ridge. At its crest we turned north and climbed for a few hundred yards towards the great towers of Dorje Lakpa itself, until we were brought to a standstill by a deep cleft. This seemed a good place in which to pause and take account of our surroundings.

To our joy we found ourselves looking right down on the very head of the Langtang Khola, facing the peaks and little glaciers at the northern end of Tilman's Panch Pokhari ridge, and with a good view of the lower part of two bigger glaciers west of Dorje Lakpa. Moreover, there before us lay what looked to be a perfectly good high-level route from the Jugal to the Langtang. At our end it entailed some tricky climbing, but as far as we could see it would " go " without a doubt. We bitterly regretted that we had not brought up more food. If we had done so, we would have changed our plans forthwith and spent a few days reconnoitring it. As it was we had no option but to go back the way we had come. We cursed ourselves heartily, and the thought of that intriguing route still haunts us like a sin of omission.

After taking photographs and bearings until the clouds put a stop to our activities, we left the ridge and returned to camp. Mingma had signalled to Kusung and Bahu from quite a long way off with the piercing Sherpa whistle, and when we arrived the kettle was whistling merrily in reply. They had also stewed us some dried peaches which we thought at first was rather an eccentric choice of food to go with tea, but it turned out to be just the dish for tired and thirsty people and went down very well.

We broke camp, intending to descend to the glacier and spend the night among the boulders again. But the march back was on the whole so easy and pleasant that we reached the glacier much earlier than we had expected. It had started to snow by now and our previous camp-site looked distinctly inhospitable. We decided, as the Sherpas were willing, to go right on to base camp.

The return journey up to our pass was a long, long pull, but we took it quietly and steadily and reached the summit of the pass more quickly and less painfully than we had anticipated. We rested there a few minutes, but since it was snowing heavily there was no inducement to sit about. The descent of the rocks on the eastern side was slightly complicated by the presence of a layer of wet snow, but once off them we lost no time in scampering down the last thousand feet and so back to dear Pomba Serebu.

The next day was spent in sorting and packing, writing up diaries and checking our films. We were inconsolable at the thought that we might be leaving Pomba Serebu, the place of peace, for ever. We had been so happy there and it was so beautiful. Imagine having Switzerland to oneself, with no tourists, and the nearest local inhabitant three days' march down the valley—that is what it was like to be at Pomba Serebu. The place had been ours; the flowers were ours, and the stream and the lochan, and the boulders, their shapes become as familiar to us as the architecture of our own homes. The cry of the " Tilling " as they flew overhead or perched on the rocks above and peered down at us in the early morning was a sound we would as lief have kept on hearing all our lives. The weird clucking and whirring of the woodcock (or *pam-toktok*, as the Tempathang Sherpas called it) at dawn and dusk still stirred us as strangely as when we had first heard it, and we had not heard enough of it. Call our attitude escapist if you like. It probably was. But it is hard to abandon paradise without a pang, and we certainly did not succeed in doing so, even though we had families we loved to return to.

In the afternoon the first of the Tempathang Sherpas arrived—a small, gnome-like man who was very polite but seemed rather at a loss as to why he was there at all. We came to the conclusion that Nima Lama had happened upon him in the forest and advised him to go to Pomba Serebu, where he would hear of something to his advantage.

Later on the rest of the porters recruited by Nima Lama came in. Nima Lama himself had taken the food boxes we had left at Tempathang up to his yak pasture, which was on the route to Panch Pokhari. Betty and I received the newcomers with glum resignation because their arrival seemed to set the seal on our impending departure. They were full of lively Sherpa chatter, and the camp rang with their laughter. The spell was finally broken, and Pomba Serebu ceased to be the threshold of adventure and reverted to its normal and ancient role of summer yak pasture.

It was then that Betty cooked up a nefarious little plan which she eventually unfolded, finding in me a willing collaborator. Above us, among the spires and pinnacles of the ridge, there was some magnificent rock scenery, ideal for photography. In the early morning the snow of the gullies and couloirs up there would be good. It was true that they were usually bombarded by falling rock and ice later in the day, but suppose we got up really early before the sun had a chance, and had a last climb? We would, she added virtuously, undoubtedly obtain some beautiful pictures. I was quite ready to agree that we owed it to ourselves not to miss this last opportunity of capturing with our cameras yet another aspect of the Jugal. It seemed as good an excuse as any for a last climb, and we went to bed feeling happier at the thought of the morrow.

We were up at six, partook of brose and cocoa and were away by seven, leaving our rucksacks packed. Mingma promised that everything would be ready for our departure on our return and wished us luck with a sympathetic grin.

We looked up at the slopes above us and reckoned on being back within three hours. But we failed to take into account the deceptive foreshortening of snow slopes seen from below, and when we had been climbing for an hour and a half, we found that we still had a long way to go. We were now amidst very fine rock scenery, but to tell the truth I was more interested in reaching the top of the ridge by a challenging snow gully than in admiring the view. Betty seemed nothing loath—in fact we both nurtured a

private hanker to have a farewell gaze from the top of the
ridge at the Phurbi Chyachumbu. So we merrily went on
cutting steps up frozen snow lying at quite a high angle and
ignoring our consciences which whispered unavailingly that
it was time we turned back.

It was not only the fleeting of time which gave us cause
for uneasiness. The sun was hot by now, and had already
begun its destructive work among the crags. On every side
we heard the clatter of rock-fall and the tinkle and crash of
falling icicles. But we hunched our shoulders and went on
obstinately. At last I reached a heel of rock at the foot of
the gully and peered up it. There was no doubt about it
being a most tempting climb, for it reared up sharply
between its walls of rock and ended high above us in a
vertical section which we could see silhouetted against the
blue sky. The claims of conscience were filed for attention
at some indefinite future period. I cut a nice step in the
beautifully hard snow of the gully and stepped on to it.
Then I stepped hurriedly back again, and crouched behind
the heel of rock just in time as two or three large blocks of
ice whizzed without a tinkle of warning down the gully.
Betty affirmed ruefully that the gully was obviously a chute
for falling objects, and that it would be madness to go on.
I agreed, and we began to descend with alacrity.

The call of duty was heard at last, and we paused in our
descent to take the photographs for which we had come.
Betty who, luckily for the expedition, took far more interest
in photography than either Evelyn or I did, was anxious to
justify our climb here by some really good results. She took
what appeared to me to be innumerable pictures, and kept
asking me to play the part of the figure in the foreground.
In my opinion she did not always pay enough attention to
what sort of foothold the foreground offered or how sheltered
it was from cannonade from above. But I followed her

directions as co-operatively as I could until she said kindly:
" Sorry to give you so much trouble."

" No trouble," I replied with equal politeness. " Only
danger." We looked at each other and grinned. We knew
perfectly well we ought to go down, but we were enjoying
ourselves far too much.

After this I thought it was Betty's turn to be the Figure
in the Foreground, but she protested. Just a couple more
shots of that curve of snow with the pinnacle perched on
the end of it. Would I mind crossing the gully and posing
on the other side? I did mind, rather, because this was the
continuation of the gully we had planned to climb and
lethal-looking missiles were skimming down it with increasing frequency. However, I approached it obediently, if
doubtfully, and was just about to entrust myself to it when,
with a noise like the sky falling, two boulders shot by,
almost knocking me over with the wind of their passing.
Turning round, full of reproach, I asked plaintively, " Do
you *still* want me to cross? "

" Yes," she replied inexorably. I gave her a dirty look
and did as I was told. (In fairness, I must add that she
only wished me to cross, not to remain in the gully. There
was no real risk in dodging across quickly, but implying
that there was makes a better story.)

The photography session over, we could think of no
further reason for prolonging our sojourn there. In any
case our spines had begun to tingle with uncomfortable anticipation whenever we turned our backs on the crags, and
we felt instinctively that it would be a wise thing to get out
while the going was good. Fortunately, the going *was*
good, and we had a splendid glissade all the way down to
the scree. In fact we came down so fast that in spite of the
time we had spent among the pinnacles we were not so
late in returning after all, and reached Pomba Serebu at

about 10.30 a.m. There we were greeted with cheerful salaams, tea, and an excellent breakfast, consisting of Mingma's special cheese omelettes with bacon and fried potatoes. After this we had only to put on our rucksacks, for base camp had been dismantled and packed up in our absence.

We kissed our hands in melancholy and affectionate farewell to Pomba Serebu, and set off down the hill after the laden train of Sherpa lads. We had forgotten how long and steep the climb up had been, and were quite surprised at the time it took us to descend. We reckoned it to be a good three thousand feet. Our downward path was decked with masses of wild irises growing in the grass, which were so pretty that we could not help being a little cheered by the sight of them.

At last we saw the green meadow of Pemsal far below, and soon were able to make out a group of people—Evelyn's party, waiting for us. When we met there was a great exchange of news, with everyone talking at once, till the threat of rain caused us to turn our attention to putting up the tents. This accomplished, Betty, Evelyn and I sheltered from the thunderstorm in the Palomine, and, with the map spread out between us, tried to sort out and interpret all our impressions of the topography of the Jugal Himal.

This is Evelyn's story as she told it to us then:

She and her party had left base camp soon after we did, and descended to Pemsal, where they paused for the Sherpas to gather plants, some to cook as a vegetable, and some for medicinal use. Setting off again, they crossed the Rakhta Khola by an airy bridge which consisted of a single tree-trunk, and camped for the night in the heart of the woods. The following day they climbed steeply to the edge of the snowline and pitched the tents on a little alp at an altitude of about 16,000 feet.

East and West

On the morning of the third day Evelyn, accompanied by Ang Temba, left camp at 7.00 a.m. for the climb to the top of the ridge. They first ascended a snow-covered rib directly above the camp, from which they traversed on to steep snowfields. They took it in turns to kick steps up and up, all the way to a narrow col on the ridge. Ang Temba was leading as they approached the col, but he suddenly paused, and with a broad grin indicated that Evelyn should go ahead and thus be the first to set foot on the crest of the ridge. It was a pretty piece of courtesy—the sort of gesture which seemed to come naturally to our Sherpas.

On the other side of the col more snow-slopes dropped steeply down to the Nosem Khola. Facing them across the valley was the frontier ridge itself, which made a right-angle turn east of Phurbi Chyachu and ran southwards for a few miles, parallel with the Chaksil Danda ridge on which Evelyn and Ang Temba now stood. Unfortunately they were too far south to see the glacier which the Nosem Khola drained.

They reached the col at 9.30, and proceeded to climb in a northerly direction up a rock and snow ridge to their left. This led them to a summit which Evelyn reckoned to be nearly 18,000 feet high. She deduced this from the fact that a peak opposite on the frontier ridge did not look to be much higher than hers and was marked on the map as 18,500. They were on top by 10.30 and stopped to take bearings, build a cairn, and plant one of the little orange route-marking flags. She christened it " *Bidean Nam Nighean,*" the hill of the maiden.

By eleven o'clock the sun was completely blotted out and the day had turned dull and cold. They climbed carefully back down the ridge until they saw a little snow gully leading down to the open snowfields below. With considerable caution they crossed several rock flakes, thinly covered with ice which was liable to peel off at each stroke of the axe. Once in the gully Evelyn glissaded down, to Ang Temba's amusement. Though a strong and agile climber, he was decidedly inexperienced and had never glissaded before. Evelyn had not realised this till she saw him follow hesitatingly and lose his balance half-way, leaving his ice-axe stuck in the snow. He managed to stop himself, and climbed back to retrieve the axe—only to repeat the performance all over again. This time Evelyn went back for the ice-axe herself and gave the Sherpa a demonstration of its correct use when glissading. Once he had grasped the principle he began to enjoy himself, and the two of them swooped down nearly a thousand feet of perfect snow to the accompaniment of shrieks of joy from Ang Temba.

The sight of this triumphant return filled Lakpa, the Tempathang Sherpa lad, with envy. That evening Evelyn saw him setting off up a nearby snow slope armed with a piece of cardboard. On this he presently seated himself and began to glide rather slowly down. Evelyn suggested that the lid of the largest *dekshi* (cooking pot) would make a better toboggan. Delighted with the idea, Lakpa set off again with the lid. It slid beautifully—faster than Lakpa had bargained for—and he shot down in a flurry of snow, looking a trifle alarmed. However, he persevered, and kept the rest of the party highly entertained by his antics for an hour or so.

Visibility was poor the next day, so, feeling that there was nothing more to be done in the time available, Evelyn decided to return at a leisurely pace to Pemsal to await our party. She had enjoyed herself enormously, and who would not, with companions such as hers. To be accompanied by the irrepressible Ang Temba, little Ang Droma with her sweet smile, good-natured Murari, sagacious

Chhepala, and Lakpa, our number two comedian, was itself an insurance against loneliness. Though she was the only member of the group who was not an Asiatic, no gulf divided her from them. It was, she told us afterwards, like a family party. Her private adventure was not only a successful, but a merry one.

Ang Temba enacted the unfamiliar roles of sirdar and cook with great enthusiasm, and produced for Evelyn meals memorable for the eccentricity of both their timing and their flavour. The highlight of these was scrambled eggs made with sugar instead of salt. Murari too became imbued with the prevailing high spirits. He had long since shed the little affectations of the city and the Sherpas liked him, though he was often the butt of their jests. One of their favourite gambits, when they were loading up in the mornings on the march, was to go to his little rucksack and pretend to have great difficulty in lifting it from the ground; staggering and crying out: " *Herteri*! Here's a heavy one! " One day Lakpa, who always carried Murari's great " *bistra* " or bedding-roll, rushed busily up to him as we were preparing to leave a camp, snatched up his rucksack, put it on, and pointing to the bed-roll cried out in Nepali, " Come on, up with your load, we have no time to lose." Murari just grinned and waited till his rucksack was returned. He and Lakpa became great friends on this trip with Evelyn, and shared his wee tent for the rest of the journey. Lakpa, who looked about fourteen, was actually eighteen, married, and a man of property, though I must say his responsibilities did not seem to weigh on him very noticeably.

The latter part of the day of reunion at Pemsal was spent in sorting out food supplies with Mingma and giving away quite a lot of surplus stores to the men to lessen weight.

Afterwards the money-box was brought out and Evelyn, in her role of treasurer, paid over advances in silver to the Tempathang Sherpas.

The weather cleared that evening, but became rather cold, and we gathered round the cooking-fire. Some of the Tempathang men joined us there, but the others were engrossed in a most exciting gambling game, the rules of which we could not fathom. There was evidently a good deal of patter connected with it, as in Crap. They were playing for cigarette points, and we recognised the brand of cigarettes we had bought for our climbing Sherpas in Kathmandu. None of them smoked except for Bahu, who had one occasionally. They had promptly sold their share to the Tempathang men, thus capitalising on our ignorance of their personal habits and the tradition that all expeditions provide free cigarettes for their climbing Sherpas. The ones who do not smoke do rather well out of this!

CHAPTER SIXTEEN

To Panch Pokhari

W E LEFT Pemsal with another loud rending of heart-strings. It was a delectable place. The previous evening Ang Droma had taken it into her head to tie bunches of rhododendrons to our tent poles, and in the fresh morning sunlight the flower-decked camp wore a festal air. But all too soon the tents were dismantled and the flowers left to wilt as we departed from the gentle meadow.

We followed the forest path which never strayed far from the river, past the landmarks of the journey up; the great cave; the moss-grown fallen trees with steps cut into their trunks, and the yak camps, now deserted, their occupants having presumably moved upwards with the melting of the snows. Flowers grew in profusion, particularly a delicate mauve tree-orchid. The Sherpas pulled bamboo shoots as they went, and gathered wild garlic. Bahu also picked flowers for Evelyn, who had collected a few to look up later in her wild flower book, and suddenly found herself with an *embarras de richesse* as he entered into the spirit of the thing and brought her great handfuls of every blosssom in sight.

When we reached the junction of the Pulmutang with the Rakhta Khola, below the great gorge, we found our bridge washed away, and had to build a new one. This did not take long, as Sherpas have light-hearted ideas about the amount of support—moral or otherwise—a heavily laden human being needs for crossing a swiftly flowing stream. We were soon across and making for the settlement with the *gompa*, where we had camped on the way up.

This time we did not stop to camp in the park-like forest adjoining the settlement, preferring to push on to another camp-site on the river below. This preference turned out to be mistaken, as it happened, because the midges were very bad by the river, while the *gompa* clearing appeared to be quite free of them.

As soon as we reached the little settlement our Sherpas dumped their loads and vanished into one of the houses, shouting for *chang*. We sat down on the grass and prepared resignedly to wait. After a while Mingma brought us out a consolation prize in the form of a brass bowl full of *chang*. We had not seen it served in this fashion before, as it is generally kept in a deep container and sucked up through a bamboo tube. In our opinion *chang* was not improved by exposure to the light of day. Its appearance, grey and murky, with bits of millet and other foreign bodies floating in the liquid, was uninviting in the extreme. The only thing to do was to close one's eyes while drinking it, and to close one's teeth as well, to form a strainer.

Having finished our share of the *chang* we began to get impatient. A few drops of rain fell, and this seemed a good excuse for sending a message into the bar that it was time to leave. Bahu, who had remained with us, conveyed the message. Ang Droma, I fear, had gone after the *chang* with the boys. Bahu returned with Kusung, with whom a little liquor went a long way, reducing him rapidly to cheerful clownishness, and Chhepala, who never drank much, though what he did drink did not affect him at all. It is interesting to note that Chhepala, who had carried on

To Panch Pokhari

Everest, apparently had a reputation for being moody and difficult. We never once saw that side of his character. He was silent, it is true, and unobtrusive, but we always found him very intelligent and sensible and absolutely reliable. In fact, I believe conditions would have been much more chaotic on the return march than they actually were if it had not been for Chhepala's sense of duty. We noticed that the other Sherpas always called him " Au Chhepala," using the honorific when they addressed him. Given the opportunity I think he might become a good sirdar.

We now left for the river, a depleted party, and descended the precipice with the aid of the tree-trunk ladders. We crossed the Langtang Khola just above its confluence with the Balephi, by the sturdy log bridge, and made for the meadow we remembered on its far side. We were sadly disappointed to find that this was not the smooth green haugh of our recollection, but a large potato field, with just one rough and vegetatious corner left uncultivated. However, we did not feel like retracing our footsteps, so decided to make camp in the uncultivated area. Chaos ensued. Half the tents had not yet arrived, and the ones that had were carried by rather intoxicated Sherpas, who wandered about tripping over things. Millions of midges attacked us, adding to the confusion. At last Mingma arrived with the rest of the party, but he was in a convivial mood, prepared to overlook inefficiency, and camp was put up in a thoroughly haphazard manner.

In the evening we emerged from our tents for supper into a cloud of vicious midges. Our only recourse was to take shelter in the choking smoke of the camp fire, which the Sherpas fed with green stuff. Here we had a very good meal of curried " weeds," potatoes and bamboo shoots. We stayed on beside the fire until quite late into the night, talking to the Sherpas and Murari. Our own Sherpas were the first to retire to bed, but the Tempathang men stayed on, chins cupped in hands, insatiable in their questions. They kept saying to Murari, "Ask them some more questions and tell us what they say." We ourselves found the conversation, which ranged from the theory and practice of speech therapy to the peculiarities of the British climate, quite absorbing. The Sherpas were very good company and we thoroughly enjoyed the evening.

The next day we followed the Balephi down towards Tempathang. But, several miles above the village, we turned off up a rough track which led very steeply uphill through thickets of dwarf bamboo and prickly undergrowth, and past an occasional potato patch. It was extremely hot and we did not enjoy this day's march at all. At last we came to a scruffy little camp-site on a sloping patch of dusty grass beside a potato field. We had to stop here, because there was in the vicinity a spring which, though fast drying up, was just large enough to provide water for drinking, though not for washing. The next spring was half a day's march away up the mountainside. This place, or rather a group of huts a little farther on, was Nima Lama's yak pasture, and he was there to greet us with his handsome and dignified lady wife and a large bottle of *rakhsi*. Mingma settled down with great celerity to drink a toast with them, while we were constrained to sip politely out of a beautiful wooden drinking-bowl lined with silver.

In the meantime camp was up, the tents all huddled together on the tiny scrap of available space. It was most uncomfortable. The midges of the previous camp had been replaced by flies and dust in this one, and to add to our afflictions a crowd of Sherpas, mostly women and children, and many of them wives and offspring of our porters, descended on us from the nearby yak pastures. Some of the yaks came too. We were clustered round and stared at all the afternoon, to the accompaniment of a great deal of hawking and spitting. Betty was able to obtain some privacy for a while by zipping herself up in her tent, but Evelyn and I were in the Palomine, which was more difficult to close completely. I hope we gave them their money's worth. Evelyn had got hold of some nuts, her favourite diet, and she ate these all the afternoon, to the admiration of the audience, who had probably never seen any one woman eat so much at one time. In the evening Evelyn held a surgery, and the audience congregated round the medicine chest, feverishly thinking up symptoms as they noted the attractive nostrums being doled out to those who were genuinely in need of them. The aspirins were in great demand, being wrapped in gleaming gold foil, which was really very pretty. As a matter of fact Evelyn said there were only two people who had anything seriously the matter with them—an old man and a baby. The rest of them looked pretty healthy on the whole, particularly the women, whose red polished cheeks were well rubbed with butter, and whose braided hair had evidently received the same treatment. In fact the dominant smell in camp that day was of rancid butter.

We were presented with cheese, eggs, potatoes, and a great deal of yak's milk, which we had to swallow with expressions of satisfaction before an audience all agog to see us enjoying the revolting stuff. Still, we were most grateful for their generosity. What friendly souls the Sherpas are! We were shocked to find that the tiny spring was the sole water supply, not only for our gang, but for the rest of the community also. Considering this, the hospitable welcome we received was all the more surprising and heartwarming.

We were awakened early by the sound of a baby crying. Our visitors were with us again in full force, and the scene of packing up camp was likened by Betty to that of a street accident in Glasgow. There were even little boys up trees, straining to catch a glimpse of our fascinating activities. Eventually, to our great relief, we were ready to move off, amid the cheerful farewells of a crowd of enthusiastic well-wishers. Our only fear, by no means a groundless one, was that they should decide to accompany us. However, they did not, and we were away at last, breasting slopes as steep and prickly as those of the day before.

Later on we found ourselves back among the cool evergreens, where we made much better progress. At last our path, such as it was, debouched on to an open hillside dotted with " ghost " trees burned out by forest fires. Above this grassy shoulder rose a long, steep, narrow ridge or spur. The route to Panch Pokhari followed the crest of this spur, the Tempathang Sherpas told us, and the last water between where we stood and the five lakes themselves was to be found, they hoped, in a small spring among the rhododendrons about a mile away. Apparently this spring often dried up completely in hot weather, so there was some doubt as to whether there would be any water at all for the night's camp. The Sherpas, who had never before made the journey to Kathmandu via Panch Pokhari at this time of year, spoke of the possibility of finding snow higher up to use for water if the spring was dry. We discounted this. Panch Pokhari itself was no higher than 13,000 feet, and the snowline was now considerably higher than that. However, distant shouts of triumph from two men who had gone on to prospect informed us that water had been found and a minor crisis averted.

We now took a path which left the bare hillside for the shelter of rhododendron forest, and led us down to a hollow among the trees where we found a small puddle holding about a basinful of very thick yellow water, almost solid with clay. After inspecting it, Evelyn gave it as her opinion that the water should be just the thing for anyone suffering from diarrhoea. This prompted us to further flights of fancy, such as the possibility of the clay lining our intestines and there hardening, leaving us with earthenware plumbing. In such case, we decided, we should have to give up mountaineering for fear that a fall would crack our internal pottery.

A little way beyond the spring we came to a delightful camp-site, a grassy clearing in the forest, where wild rhubarb grew plentifully. As soon as the tents were put up all hands fell to picking the rhubarb. We asked Mingma to stew us some for supper. He did so, but he also gave us some prepared Sherpa-fashion—chopped up raw and mixed with salt, chillies and yak's-milk cottage-cheese. Either way, it was delicious. The clayey water, when mingled with milk powder, looked so like café-au-lait that the only possible additions to it were sugar and coffee powder. This made a very good drink, with plenty of body to it.

That evening a furious quarrel arose between Kusung and Tensing Lama, one of the Tempathang men, over a groundsheet which had been left behind at Pemsal. Each said this piece of expedition property had been the responsibility of the other. Tensing Lama, a man of volatile temperament, was hysterical with fury, and screamed accusations and abuse at Kusung, who just sat grinning maddeningly and making provocative remarks every time Tensing Lama paused for breath. The quarrel went on and on, with Mingma occasionally putting in soothing interpolations and the rest of the party listening with interest. Tensing Lama was so terribly angry and accompanied his undoubtedly unbridled language with such vulgar noises and gestures, that we began to wonder whether

we ought to intervene. However, just as the row was at its
height and Kusung had goaded his antagonist into a state
of spluttering rage that looked as if he would have to either
do him bodily harm or burst, an unattended pressure-
cooker suddenly exploded in such an appropriate manner
that we all began to laugh. The tension was relieved, the
opponents fell silent, looking rather shamefaced, and peace
returned to the camp.

Dawn greeted us with an unexpected and breathtaking
vision of the Jugal Himal, and we dived for our cameras.
But to our disappointment the superb view was quickly
blotted out by mist. At seven o'clock nothing more could
be seen, and the unpleasant dampness of the weather gave
us no cause for idling. We were away by seven-thirty,
climbing steeply back to the crest of the spur. Once up,
we had a delightful ridge-walk which lasted several hours.
The only fault we could find with the march this day was
that the mist hid our surroundings, and gave us the curious
sensation of walking the plank above an ocean of grey cloud.
The Tempathang men, who knew exactly how long it would
take to get to Panch Pokhari, kept stopping to rest and
chat. We pushed on impatiently, partly because all we
knew about the day's journey was that we had a long way
to go, and partly because we soon grew chilly sitting waiting
for the men. At one period Ang Droma decided to lead,
and scurried ahead, a comic little figure with a load nearly
as big as herself which did not appear to inconvenience her
at all. She pushed through long grass and undergrowth
like some small wild creature, and clambered nimbly over
the rocks. The path was invisible most of the time, but we
just followed the crest of the spur, sometimes having to
literally hack our way through the bushes with kukris.
Mingma exclaimed disapprovingly that this route was
" *Bahut zungle,*" very wild. Wait till we reach Panch

Pokhari, he told me. From there on the path would be big enough to take a yak.

At one of our stops I introduced Ang Droma to an old game of my childhood, " Open your mouth and shut your eyes and see what the king has sent you." This was easily translated into Nepali, and was played in this case with bits of mint cake and chocolate. Both the game and the food went down well.

At last the route left the spur and traversed the hillside below it. The Tempathang men now seemed to be divided in their opinion as to the exact route, and, since the mist was thicker than ever, we began to wonder whether we ever would reach Panch Pokhari that day. I was not reassured by hearing Lakpa, who was forging ahead and who we were following, chant a ditty to himself which ran something like this: " I have lost the path. But never mind. I don't speak English. But never mind . . ." It was just as well, I thought, that I could not understand any more of it.

" Has he really lost the path? " I asked Murari, who questioned one of the Tempathang lads.

" They say he's always losing the path," he replied, with a grin.

Fortunately, another Tempathang boy, altogether a more serious-minded type, now announced that he was on the correct path. This led us over a shoulder to the lip of a cup or hollow containing a stream and a small lochan. So there *was* water to be found before Panch Pokhari, though it was certainly a long way from our camp of the previous night. We stopped to eat our " pieces " on the lip of the hollow, and then descended into it for a drink. It was filled with a fluffy-leaved plant with a long tuberous root. The Sherpas dug these up, peeled the roots and ate them. They gave us some. The root had the consistency of raw turnip and the flavour of rather tasteless coconut.

A little of it went a long way, a fact that the Sherpas themselves admitted. They also dug up the roots of a plant which looked like an orchid of sorts. These they dry and grind to make a febrifuge.

It was in this hollow that we found the nest and fledgelings of a tiny wren. We went into hiding and waited for the mother to return. She was very cautious about it, circling the nest, and creeping towards it under the grass like a wee mouse. And no wonder, with Ang Temba giving an elaborate pantomime of bird-watching behind a nearby boulder. As soon as she popped into the nest he proved that her suspicions were justified by leaping out and placing his hand over the opening, imprisoning her. We told him off indignantly, and he went away whistling with his hands in his pockets like a naughty boy.

As soon as we climbed out of the hollow we found ourselves exposed to driving hail and sleet. Very raw and nasty it was. The weather and our surroundings reminded us irresistibly of the Scottish hills. The country around us (what we could see of it) looked like moorland, which would undoubtedly be lovely in good weather, but under these conditions was rather bleak and unwelcoming. After about an hour of battling upwards against the gale, we found ourselves on top of the Panch Pokhari ridge. As far as we could see, which was not far, we were on a rolling moor, a plateau dotted with outcrops of rock, across which ran a meagre trace of a path. All that was missing was heather and peat-hags.

The three of us had kept together and had at some time on the way up been joined by Kusung, Ang Droma, Murari and Lakpa, though it was doubtful as to who was leading whom. In the mist we became separated from the rest of the party, and when the path appeared to peter out Lakpa, for want of anyone more reliable, was called upon to lead us in the right direction. After some casting about, during which we nearly mislaid Kusung, he got us on to what looked like a path. We said we would wait in the shelter of a boulder for the rest of the party. Nonsense, nonsense, said Lakpa. He could lead us straight to Panch Pokhari. Follow me, he added, and set off into the mist. We remained where we were and shouted to him to wait. After a minute we heard him call out in beseeching accents that he could *see* a *pokhara*. "Is it nice?" shouted Murari mockingly. Deeply hurt, Lakpa rejoined us. The rest of the party loomed up shortly afterwards and we all went on together. Lakpa had certainly got us back on the right track, but as certainly he had not seen a *pokhara*. The path led us up to a saddle marked with a cairn, and not until we began to descend on its far side could anyone have seen the gleam of water. At last we were within the basin in which lie the Panch Pokhari, the five lakes regarded by Nepal Hindus as sacred to the god Shiva.

The Sherpas shouted with triumph and began to run downhill, only stopping to pick up sticks and bits of brushwood. The mist was so thick that we came right to the edge of the first pokhara quite unexpectedly. It was an exciting moment.

We made camp on a grassy mound between two of the pokhari and then all split up to go wood-foraging. As the afternoon advanced the mist cleared and the sun came out. We found Panch Pokhari well worth waiting for. Imagine a basin, its rim consisting of a circle of small crags, containing five separate and exquisite lochs, divided by green and grassy mounds. I say lochs, because the whole place was so like a bit of the Highlands. Betty said that the moment she set eyes on it she heard the pipes.

Evelyn and I went to join Mingma, who had gone off with the field-glasses to spy out our route for the next day.

We found ourselves above the Indrawati river, which has its source in the five lochs, and looking at the Nauling Lekh from the north-west. Our path led southwards along a ridge which joined the Nauling Lekh, and from where we stood we could see all the way to our next camp-site, a distant green patch where the Tempathang men said water was to be found. Having settled this, we went on to look at the little Shiva " temple." This was a small shrine built of stones, surrounded by heaps of iron tridents, symbols of the god carried thither by devout pilgrims at the annual festival, which occurs in July, a time when water is certain to be found on the Nauling Lekh. Murari, a good Hindu, and one of the Sherpas, who should have been a good Buddhist but seemed to think it wiser to propitiate " whatever gods there be," began to dance clockwise round the shrine. Evelyn followed, while I watched her with some amusement. When she was half-way round I said, " Shiva is the god of reproduction, you know. Women who wish to be blessed with pregnancy go round the temple as you're doing." Evelyn stopped short in some alarm and rapidly retraced her footsteps. " Come on," she said. "I've got to undo the spell. We'll circumnavigate all the Panch Pokhari anti-clockwise, to make sure." She set off at great speed. I went with her in the role of witness in case it came to an argument with Shiva. However, he must have been convinced, we think, by our prompt counter-move. It was certainly a long walk round the five lochs, and by the time we had completed the tour the mist had enveloped us once more.

That night we talked for a long time in the Palomine. Our spirits had risen steadily as we gained altitude, and this was our happiest evening since we left Pomba Serebu.

N.B. See map on p. 51 for our return route *via* Panch Pokhari.

228

CHAPTER SEVENTEEN

The Demon Chang

THE NEXT morning was so cold that the zip of my tent, water-logged the night before, was frozen and I had some difficulty in getting out. The day was clear and sunny, but some suspicious-looking clouds were already appearing over the rim of the basin. Without waiting for breakfast, Betty, Evelyn and I dressed quickly and set off towards the cairn on the " pass " to take photographs. We had great hopes of seeing the Jugal Himal in panorama and of being close enough to the mountains to be able to confirm all the impressions gathered during our explorations there. I went on ahead at a run, because I felt quite sure that the clouds were coming up fast. It was not possible to see the mountains from the pass, so I ran round the top of the rim of the basin until I reached a point from which the Jugal Himal could be clearly seen. Unfortunately, they had already gathered to themselves a screen of clouds. I did take some photographs, but my heart was not in the job, as the results subsequently showed. Then I went slowly down to the camp again, too homesick for the mountains to stay and talk about them to the others. When Betty and Evelyn got to the same point they wisely waited in the hope that the clouds would shift sufficiently to enable them to take some worthwhile pictures. This is just what happened, and some fairly good shots of the Jugal and one or two excellent ones of Panch Pokhari rewarded their patience.

But there was nothing new to be learned about the Jugal from what it was possible to see that day.

The bungalow tent had been left up at our request for use as a bathroom. We took turns in washing in it and changing into garments more suitable for the warmth of the journey back to Kathmandu. This meant discarding our invaluable string vests, which had been our second skins. I felt as if I had moulted suddenly when I rolled mine up and shoved it, with a sigh, into my kitbag. Emerging spotless, we went down to the largest *pokhara* to wash our hair. Very cold indeed it was, so cold that it gave us temporary neuralgia, which, however, responded to treatment. The treatment consisted of an enormous breakfast—cheese omelette, potatoes, biscuits and marmalade.

Knowing their propensity for sitting about, we sent the Sherpas on ahead, only Mingma, Murari, Nima Lama and Bahu remaining with us. At about 10.15 a.m. we set off reluctantly for Panch Pokhari was too enchanting a spot to be left easily. We followed the path " big enough for a yak," and came to the conclusion that Mingma's yaks must be more active than most. This path began by making a long scrambling descent, which was very disheartening, because we could see Chang Samaphu ahead of us, looking quite high, and we knew that our next camp was half-way up it. After about an hour's walk we caught up the rest of the party, who had adopted their favourite recumbent positions, and all went on together. At first we traversed hillsides in thick mist, but later this cleared and we had a wonderful day walking along narrow ridges, the valley of the Indrawati on our right and that of the Balephi on our left. The hillsides were clad with shrub rhododendrons, all in flower. Murari and I rather wantonly picked big bunches of them though we knew that they would not last. We simply could not resist the more unusual shades of mauve and purple, nor the pure bridal-white blossoms. In the late afternoon we came to a stretch of green turf, which Nima Lama said was the camp-site we had been making for. Mingma went off to look for water, while we all waited anxiously. We had known that finding water on the top of the Nauling Lekh would be a chancy business in the hot weather, and would not have returned that way if the Tempathang Sherpas had not assured us that they knew where to find permanent springs.

A series of shrill whistles told us that our faith in the Sherpas was vindicated—so far. Mingma had found a stream. It was not near enough to the grass clearing for us to camp in the open, so we went on to join Mingma and made camp in a pleasant sloping glade in the rhododendron forest. There was plenty of water in the stream—even a little waterfall—and more fuel than we could possibly use. Betty and I started collecting sticks after the manner, she said, of French aristocrats milking cows at Versailles. It was a charming pastime, but unnecessary, as there was firewood to hand in every direction.

That night we made a grand big fire, and sat round it even while the rain came pattering down through the trees and hissed in the embers.

The following morning was warm, and for the first time for many weeks, we did not feel averse to climbing out of our sleeping-bags. Nima Lama led the way once more, and we followed him up through the forest and over the shoulder of Chang Samaphu. A fine view of the Jugal could sometimes be obtained between the trees, but, by the time we reached the open hillside it had become somewhat obscured by cloud. All the same, we learnt more from it as to the relation of the Jugal to the Langtang and the Gaurisanker Himal, than from any other viewpoint on the march back.

Tents in the Clouds

We were now on the Nauling Lekh proper, and enjoyed all day a sunny ridge-walk at an altitude of about 10,000 feet. Flowers grew thick about our path, the most common being a largish cornflower-blue daisy. At one halt I started making a daisy-chain, and was surprised to find that this was something the Sherpa children do not do. At least, all our Sherpas, both of the Sola Khombu and the Tempathang communities, were most intrigued, and for the rest of the day making flower chains became the fashion. Even Mingma made one, though under the pretext of helping me add to mine. Ang Temba, who had no dignity to stand on, went in for the new craze in a big way, hanging chains of flowers from neck, ears, balaclava and buttonholes, till he looked like something left over from the Nice carnival.

Our merry mood began to fade when we found no water at all at the next camp-site. Never mind, said Nima Lama, there was another place only two hours' march farther on where there was *always* water. Just then we met some villagers from a hamlet lower down the hillside, who had been cutting canes in the forest. When questioned, they scoffed at the idea of our finding any water at all on our route. Our hearts sank, but there was nothing for it but to go on and hope for the best.

The camp-site, when we reached it, was unalluring. On a bare hillside stood two long roofless shelters for pilgrims, and about half a mile from them was a place by the path where a few cupfuls of muddy liquid had oozed out of a bank into a hole about as big as a soup-plate. This was our water supply, and even the most sanguine Sherpa could not but realise that it was inadequate, to say the least, for a party of our size. Everybody immediately began to feel very thirsty.

The first thing to do was to see just how much the spring would yield. We drained it dry and rationed the water.

The Demon Chang

It worked out at about a quarter of a cupful for each person, with none for cooking. Cross and complaining, the Sherpas put up the tents. They chose to put them up inside the shelters, though I for one did not care for this idea at all. But I felt too depressed to argue. Altogether the spirits of the expedition were at a low ebb.

Nevertheless, one member of the party was able to extract some entertainment from our predicament. There was nothing Ang Temba enjoyed more than a nice little disaster. Nothing serious, of course, but just any incident involving a certain amount of discomfiture all round. On this occasion, he came to the front of our tents, to find the mem-sahibs gloomily sucking boiled sweets for want of anything better to do. Briskly he set the " table " with mugs and plates, biscuits, sardines and jam, pulling knives, spoons and forks out of the various pockets in which he always conveyed them to us at meal-times. Then he drew himself up and in the very voice which he generally used for his chant of " Tea? Coffee? " etc., he announced, " Mem-sahib, No tea! No coffee! No orange ju'! No Horli'! No Marmite! No cocoa! " Before he could finish, the humour of the situation overcame him to such an extent that he slapped his thigh and laughed till he cried. So infectious was his good humour that we too saw the jest and began to laugh with him. Dear Ang Temba!

Sherpas do not easily accept defeat, and the Tempathang men had no intention of going to bed without their rice if they could help it. Some of them set off down the hillside to find a village, and eventually came to one about two miles away. There they filled a can with water and returned triumphant. Seeing this Mingma immediately sent Bahu down, not only with our largest water, carrying can, but with the hot-water bottle, both of which receptacles he brought back full, to everyone's joy, gratitude and relief.

He also brought back a frog, concealed in a tin, which the Sherpas invited me to open, doubtless hoping to elicit a satisfying reaction. However, I like frogs, so they got no change out of me. What is more, I was prepared to handle it, which they themselves were not. Betty and Evelyn were equally unobliging, and though Bahu went the rounds with the poor beastie, the only person with whom his joke really succeeded was Ang Droma, who let out a shriek and retreated, to the dishonour of her sex.

Evelyn and I were aroused in the morning by exclamations from Betty, and came out of our tents to see a glorious sight. The whole of the Jugal and the Langtang Himalaya hung in the sky above the summit of Chang Samarphu like a magnificent frieze. We took photographs and discussed and pointed out landmarks to each other. We could even see the mountain we had climbed, a tiny bubble appearing behind Dorje Lakpa and The Big White Peak, which we regarded with a mixture of affection and deprecation as if it was, Betty said, a rather *déclassé* poor relation.

It was a beautiful day, and once more, the march was pure pleasure most of the way, though it began to get uncomfortably hot in the afternoon as the heights of the Nauling Lekh dwindled and dropped away towards Okhreni. This was the Sherpa settlement near where we had made our third camp on the march out to Tempathang, before we turned east towards the Belephi Khola. When we came in sight of the village, Mingma, followed by other Sherpas, dashed ahead in a purposeful manner. Was he going on in advance to set up camp and make tea? He was not. He was hot on the track of *chang*. We three, with Murari, went on through the village and through a stretch of rhododendron forest, where we were glad to see several swiftly flowing streams, to the "*maidan*" which had been the site of our camp the last time. Here, deserted by everyone but our faithful Murari, we waited for over two hours. We had expected to wait for some time, because there was no reason at all why the Sherpas should not refresh themselves, but this was a bit much. When he did arrive, explaining that he had remained to round up stragglers who would otherwise have still been in the *chang* house, our sirdar had to talk pretty fast to get on the right side of the three irate memsahibs. We did not thaw easily, either, though if we had not felt so hot, thirsty and indignant, the scene around us would have struck us as irresistibly funny.

On the advice of the Sherpas we had moved up to a higher maidan, which was cooler. This place turned out to be a sort of local Piccadilly Circus. Villagers kept crossing it on their way home from the hillsides, carrying bundles of sticks, grass or leaves, and driving their flocks and herds before them. To a man, woman or child they stopped to stare, while their livestock wandered freely round the camp. It was pandemonium. There were goats entangled in the guy-ropes, babies crawling into the tents, and buffaloes in the soup. Dogs barked, slightly intoxicated Sherpas waved their arms vaguely at the intruders, and a cloud of dust hung over everything. Kusung, sent to chase the audience a little farther from our tents, lined them up and delivered to them an oration, the gist of which was that he was a Sherpa from Sola Khombu, where men were men, and mountaineers to boot. We gathered from his gestures that he went on to relate how he and his colleagues had saved the day on many an awesome glacier and peak. There was a good deal of barracking, and interjections which were unmistakably the Nepali equivalent of " Tell that to the marines." The whole situation was so farcical and Kusung so splendidly comic that it was too much for our gravity. We broke down and laughed.

Seeing that we had relaxed and were once more approachable, Mingma forthwith approached. Those Tempathang men, he said, disassociating himself from them with an expressive shrug, were complaining that the soles of their feet had been scorched by the heat of the ground. They wanted to start very early in the morning and walk till noon, no longer. Would we agree? We would certainly agree, we told him, if they, in their turn, would agree to keep moving and not make us wait for hours on end. Mingma, who obviously had not expected us to acquiesce so readily, grinned broadly and said that the Tempathang men would be very happy when he told them that their suggestion had been accepted. We then decided to rise at four a.m. and be on the move before 5.30.

It was a terrible night. The Sherpas must have had a supply of *chang* put by, for they shouted and yelled until past midnight, while a frenzied dog barked and barked throughout the small hours. We lay awake thinking it was just as well we had no firearms with us. The dog might have been the first to be dispatched, but there was no telling where the slaughter would have ended once begun. As it was we ground our teeth and cursed all men and dogs who kept unseasonable hours and had to let every one know about it. Four o'clock came as a blessed release, and we rose and dressed quickly, eager to see the last of that infuriating camp. We were all away soon after five, and it certainly was extremely pleasant to walk in the cool of the morning and watch the rising sun touch the mountain tops on the horizon.

We reached Nawalpur by eight and felt quite pleased with our progress and with the success of this new system of early rising. But here we received a set-back. The Tempathang Sherpas, it seemed, wanted to stop in the village to arrange about food supplies for their return journey. That may have been so, but we soon became aware that there were other reasons for halting, more pressing and not entirely unconnected with the demon *chang*. One by one our henchmen slipped away, trying to look nonchalant, and disappeared into *chang* shops. Nawalpur was not a particularly salubrious place, nor did its inhabitants seem overjoyed to see us. We had got so used to being welcomed with open arms wherever we went in Nepal that this indifference seemed almost insulting. We told each other that we were now among more sophisticated people who may have seen foreigners before, but this did not really console us. We had been spoilt.

After sitting about for more than an hour, during which time the sun had begun to get very hot, and Mingma had twice come to us, requesting, on behalf of the Tempathang men, our indulgence for yet another " five minutes," we sent round an ultimatum. We intended to go on down to the Indrawati. If we were not joined there very shortly by the whole party we were going to be seriously annoyed. Having delivered ourselves of this rather unconvincing threat, we gathered up Murari, Kusung, Chhepala, Ang Droma, and one or two others who either felt the call of duty, or (more likely), had run out of money, and swept out of Nawalpur in high dudgeon. This time there was going to be no nonsense about not using the ferry. We made precise inquiries as to its whereabouts, and took the quickest route down the hill to the stretch of river across which it plied. On the way we were caught up by Mingma, Ang Temba, and some of the other Sherpas. The rest were not far behind. We hoped that it was our resolute action which had suitably impressed them.

By now the blazing sun had once more heated the hard stony ground so that it burned the soles of the Tempathang Sherpas' bare feet. Living at altitudes where it never really gets very hot, and always travelling over grassy or moss-grown paths, they are not inured to heat in the way that the villagers of the lower hills and valleys are, and they really did suffer, especially when it came to crossing the baking silver sands of the Indrawati bed. We longed to say, " I told you so," but refrained with an effort. The ferry was a dug-out canoe, operated by two men who pushed and poled it dexterously across the swift main stream. Once across this, it was still necessary to wade, or jump from stone to stone, before reaching the farther bank. As the boat only held four people with their loads at one trip, it was some time before our party was able to foregather on the far side of the river. The Tempathang Sherpas picked up their loads at once and made for the nearby village as if drawn towards it by invisible strings. It was now midday, and we were prepared to stick to our side of the bargain and make camp. But *not* beside the village. From the opposite side of the river we had seen a big tree which stood out noticeably in this arid landscape, about a mile downstream beyond the village. This we had pointed out to Mingma, Nima Lama and others as a good camp-site. They had agreed. But it looked as though the village, squatting athwart the path like temptation personified, might turn out to be another Nawalpur. " Listen," I said to Mingma, " we are *not* stopping in the village. Tell them that." " Yes, memsahib," he replied, glancing from side to side rather desperately. And well he might, for there was nobody left to tell. They had all streaked off to the *chang*-pots. I realised that poor Mingma had even less control over the Tempathang men than we had supposed. One word from him and they did as they liked. We went on towards the village, Murari causing a slight diversion by inadvertently plunging fully dressed into a tributary of the Indrawati which he was in the act of crossing.

Once through the village, Betty, Evelyn and I stopped.

The Demon Chang

We were now alone, attended only by a swarm of flies. If we went on we might have to wait for a couple of hours, as at Okhreni. If we remained where we were we might have to endure this malodorous situation for at least an hour, as at Nawalpur. We had got up long before dawn for nothing, it seemed. The injustice of this overcame me, and I determined to present our case most forcibly to the Sherpas. Telling the others that I would be back in a minute, I returned to the centre of the village. The Tempa-thang Sherpas were all sitting in a *chang* house, gazing unmoved at Murari, who was haranguing them. Mingma and our other climbing Sherpas, discreetly buying eggs and potatoes, were nowhere to be seen. Murari looked relieved when he saw me. " They won't come, Memsahib," he said, mopping his brow. " They say their feet are sore."

" Look," I said firmly, fixing the Sherpas with a reproach-ful eye, " tell them that we agreed to get up at four o'clock because we were sorry about their feet. Tell them we are willing to travel all night and sleep all day if they prefer it that way, but ask them, is it fair that they should make us lose our sleep so that they may sit about drinking *chang* until the ground gets too hot to walk upon? Tell them they can't have it both ways."

Nepali is sufficiently like Hindustani to enable me to follow Murari's translation of each sentence. It stuck closely to the original, and as he ended I held my breath, waiting to see the effect of this speech upon the Sherpas. They looked at me, then at each other with raised eyebrows. Then, to my infinite gratification, grins spread across their faces, they nodded, and rose. It was a reasonable argument and they were reasonable men. They would come. Taking no chances, I stayed with them till we reached the trees and solicitously offered round glucose tablets when we got there.

Tents in the Clouds

This camp above the Indrawati had many drawbacks. It was too close to the Kathmandu path, so that we were constantly surrounded by onlookers, asking questions, cadging cigarettes and correcting our pronunciation of place names. There were flies galore and there were mosquitoes at night. It was cramped for space and it was very hot. But it had one great advantage which outweighed them all—the river itself. In a short while the Sherpas started trickling down in twos and threes to nearby pools, our Sola Khombu men carrying such appurtenances of civilisation as soap and towels. Betty, Evelyn, Ang Droma and I were hard put to it to find a private place of our own, and had to walk a long way. When we reached a suitable stretch of water we washed our hair and then waded in and lay like buffaloes, only our noses out of the water. The memsahibs, that is. Ang Droma, who had no bathing-costume, did not immerse herself totally, though she had a good wash. Incidentally, the bathing-costumes were very necessary as the privacy of this place was only relative. The people regarded us curiously, but politely refrained from advancing to ask questions until we were fully dressed and combing our hair. Then, naturally, they descended upon us.

We returned to the camp, where we had a meal made memorable by roast chicken. We seemed to have run out of nearly everything in the main course line by now except meat bar, of which we had an apparently inexhaustible supply, and which we never wished to taste again. The chicken was small and stringy, but compared to meat bar it was a banquet in itself.

That evening Evelyn and I went swimming again, to cool ourselves down for the night. The pool we entered smelt a bit, but we were long past being choosy. To be immersed in water was enough.

The Demon Chang

The next morning we got up at 4.30 a.m. with an uncomfortable day before us. We now had to cross a last big ridge, the watershed between the valley of the Indrawati and the vale of Kathmandu. We followed a stream for a time and then climbed up and up a spur for hours. It became pretty hot, though not unbearably so, as we were making height all the time. At last we came to the top of the spur and saw the place where we had made Camp I on our outward journey. After this it was not so steep, though still as dusty and shadeless. We came to a large village where the Sherpas stopped for food and *chang*. I said to Nima Lama, " Promise not to be too long. Not more than half an hour," and showed him half an hour on my watch. He nodded, smiling in agreement. We three memsahibs went on, and stopped at a place on the path which happened to overlook the back yard of the *chang* house. We had a good view of the Sherpas eating and drinking, and felt rather envious of them. But, unlike the Sherpa settlements, these lower Nepali villages were exceedingly dirty and we had no desire to spoil our record of good health at the last moment.

When half an hour had passed, we saw Mingma trying unsuccessfully, with his cries of " Lo, lo, lo," to get the men to make a move. Hoping to be able to repeat my success of the day before, I ran back and went round to the yard of the *chang* shop. It was a scruffy place, with pools of *chang* all over the veranda and a sleeping baby lying among them, flies clustering at its eyes and nostrils. The men were drinking rice-beer, almost as thick as porridge, and probably most nutritious. They offered me some, but I replied truthfully, that I dared not, since it would make me sick in my stomach. Then I reminded Nima Lama of his promise. The Tempathang men rose like lambs and shouldered their loads. I could have embraced them, though I dare say Mingma did not see eye to eye with me in the matter. He

241

was a kindly soul who did not like to throw his weight about too much, and I think the humorous independence of the Tempathang men was a trial he had not bargained for. We could see that he was sometimes afraid that if pressed too far they would put down their loads and go home. They could be very provoking. Once when we were all ready to start and our climbing Sherpas stood up, crying, " Lo! lo! lo! " I saw one of the Tempathang lads deliberately take out a cigarette and light it. " We are not ready to go yet," he said with a smirk. " Can't you see we are smoking? " However, it seemed that a good-tempered and fairly worded request was something they understood and appreciated.

We trudged on and on, passing through villages and shadeless terraced fields bearing sturdy crops of maize, but nowhere could we see a possible camp-site. By this time the summit of the watershed, which was an uncultivated park-like plateau covered with short grass and thorny scrub, was in sight, and we wondered wistfully if we could ever persuade the Sherpas to go as far as that. I asked Nima Lama speculatively if he thought we might find water there. If so, would it not make a good camp-site? To my surprise and delight, he said that there *was* good water to be found there and that it would be an excellent place in which to camp. So, after a few more stops for *chang* (which we did not grudge, having won our point over going right on to the uncultivated ground, though it was well past midday), we came at last to the pleasant hilltop, well away from crowds and villages, and pitched the tents on a knoll near a clear stream. This camp-site bore about the same relation to Pomba Serebu or Panch Pokhari as Hampstead Heath to Rannoch Moor, but it was quiet and peaceful, and there was a good breeze. In the afternoon we brailed the Palomine and lay supine beneath its shade.

The Demon Chang

There was one matter that had to be settled that day. On the morrow we would reach the town of Sankhu, and we had no desire to find ourselves parked in the main square to be stared at while the Sherpas slaked their thirst. Nor did we intend to go on ourselves, leaving our Sherpas (and incidentally our equipment) behind. We decided that I should call a staff conference. Accordingly, I went to seek out Mingma, Murari and Nima Lama. But if I thought this was to be a private meeting with the Big Three, I was mistaken. In democratic Sherpaland there is neither caste nor class, and none of our men considered themselves to be rank and file. As soon as they saw the committee members draw aside they all came rushing up to see what was afoot, like chickens hoping to be fed. Moreover, they did not come as passive onlookers, but as fully-fledged committee members themselves. Resigning myself to the fact that this was now a public meeting, I explained, through Murari, our misgivings about Sankhu. They all nodded gravely and sympathetically, and murmurs of " Quite right, quite right," were heard. Encouraged, I went on to say that our wish was that all members of the expedition party should foregather outside Sankhu and that we should march right through the town without stopping. When Murari had finished saying all this in Nepali, Mingma repeated it in the Sherpa tongue, after which I added a postscript in Hindustani. The kind-hearted Sherpas, delighted at being confided in, more or less patted me on the back and assured me that all would be well. They would see to it personally that nobody should stare at the memsahibs in Sankhu.

They kept their word. The next morning those who had been the vanguard of the party as we descended the Kathmandu side of the watershed stopped, as soon as Sankhu came in sight, to wait for the stragglers. I took some photographs while we waited, of Mingma, Chhepala and

Ang Droma, each posing in my hat among the appreciative giggles of their friends. This hat, a sort of stitched cotton pork-pie in an unbecoming shade of khaki, had served me well during the hot days of the march. The Sherpas thought it funny, which of course it was, but what I did not realise was that they also thought it a desirable object. On the previous day, when Betty had been taking pictures of everybody, Ang Temba had asked to be photographed in the hat. We had thought it a joke, which perhaps it was, as anyway it was too small for him, but when we reached Kathmandu he went out and bought himself one exactly like it, which made him look horribly townee and spivvish. We were glad to see that he subsequently gave it to Kusung. No headgear could make Kusung look anything but the simple soul he was.

Now we were ready for the onslaught on Sankhu. Shouldering our loads and keeping together in a compact body, we approached the town at a rapid trot. The inhabitants, going about their daily business, were startled into immobility by the sight of the entire Scottish Women's Himalayan Expedition, looking neither right nor left, tearing through the streets like a scalded cat. It was a case of " That's an expedition—that was," for in a few minutes we were out of the little town again and dashing down a real road to Kathmandu. The only exception was Kusung, who carried the " eyes front " business to such lengths that he did not notice the rest of the party turning up a side street, but went on marching straight ahead. We often wondered afterwards where he would have landed up if Evelyn had not seen him disappearing and gone to his rescue.

About a mile out of the town we came to a place where the quiet road was pleasantly shaded by eucalyptus trees. The Sherpas paused. " May we stop here? " they asked. " Certainly," we said benignly, highly pleased at the success of our plan for getting past Sankhu. They dumped their loads and we all sat down in the shade. "Are you quite comfortable," somebody inquired of us. We said we were. "That's good," they said sweetly, "because now we're going back to Sankhu. We won't be long." Betty, Evelyn and I looked at each other speechless. Then the humour of the situation struck us and we began to laugh. The Sherpas had kept their word, had deposited us in a quiet and comfortable place with no crowds to stare at us. Why should they not go and have a drink? We asked them not to be more than half an hour, and passed the time quite enjoyably in the company of Mingma and Murari, who waited with us. To our surprise the others *did* come back within half an hour. Our Tempathang ruffians were honourable gentlemen.

About six miles from Kathmandu we stopped at the last possible site—a patch of grazed-down turf outside a village. It is true that we could have gone on and reached the capital that night, but for various reasons, including the fact that for fear of being met by reporters, we had refrained from sending any intimation in advance of our coming, we preferred to arrive in the morning rather than at night. So the tents were pitched for the last time, and for the last time we sat round a camp fire with the Sherpas. We decided to use up all the remaining milk, sugar and coffee powder and serve coffee and biscuits all round. The Sherpas, who could work up a party spirit on the most unpromising fare, enjoyed themselves. They smacked their lips over the coffee, ran races, and danced and sang by the fire till late into the night. The villagers, especially the children, must have thought we were a circus. They turned out *en masse* to stare and applaud.

With all these people about, Mingma developed qualms over the money-box. He brought it to me and asked me to keep it that night, as I was in a mountain tent which could be closed up completely. "Call out if anyone tries to rob you in the night," he said ominously, as he departed for the Sherpa tent. I said I would, and fished out with pride my good big sheath-knife which up to now had never been called upon to assume a more dramatic role than the dispensing of sardines. This I placed ready to hand, gleefully prepared to shed blood in the defence of our cash. However, I slept so soundly that night that I rather think a marauder could have walked off with the box and the sheath-knife as well if he had felt so inclined.

In the morning all the familiar camp equipment was packed up for the last time and we set off on the last lap of our journey. Ang Droma was so affected by our impending parting that she took Betty's hand and clung to it all the way to Kathmandu. The two of them walking side by side, tall Betty and tiny Ang Droma, made rather a touching picture.

The road we were on led past the Bodha Stupa, which we soon saw in the distance, holding us with the uncomfortably hypnotic stare of its great painted eyes. When we reached its outer gates the Sherpas stopped for food. To avoid the curious crowd which collected as soon as we stopped, we went into the inner courtyard and wandered about, looking at the prayer wheels and the carving on the houses which encircled the courtyard. Just then the Chinni Lama put his head out of a window and, seeing us, invited us in to breakfast. We were very glad to accept his hospitality and were once more vastly entertained by the conversation of his vivacious daughter. When we saw our men begin to gather in the courtyard we took our leave with many expressions of gratitude and went down to join them. Beside Mingma was a strange Sherpa who salaamed me politely. I greeted him abstractedly, not paying much

attention until he said, " Memsahib, don't you know me? "
And looking again, I saw that it was young Lakpa Gyelbu,
who had climbed with me in Sikkim. He had filled out
and grown into a man since then and I could hardly
recognise him. But I was very pleased to see him, for he
had been my special Sherpa then. We shook hands and
exchanged news of old friends.

By this time the whole party had rejoined us, in tearing
spirits and breathing forth clouds of *chang*. Before we left
the Stupa they had to make the round of it, turning the
prayer wheels. We began to follow suit, murmuring " *Om
mani padme hum.*" " That's right, memsahib," quoth
Kusung, delighted. " Do as I do." The pace became
faster and faster, till we were all rushing round, birling the
prayer wheels like mad. " Don't you think," panted Betty
in my ear, " that this is rather irreverent? " Not being a
Buddhist I could not tell her, but none of the Sherpas
seemed to think so.

Eventually the requirements of religion seemed to be
satisfied, and we picked up our packs and set off again into
the town. When we came to a cross-roads Murari indicated
one direction as being the quicker, while Mingma insisted
that the other was. Neither would give in and for a time
we seemed to have reached a deadlock. Then the party
split into factions, each prepared to follow its chosen guide.
Murari's party, in which we memsahibs found ourselves,
walked sedately down the road till Mingma's followers were
out of sight, and then with one accord began to run. We
had to prove ourselves right, you see. Of course the others
had hit upon the same idea, and as the two routes were just
about equal in distance, it turned into a race. We reached
the place where the two routes reunited at the same moment
as the others came pounding down the road, and the rival
parties converged amid shouts, jeers and laughter. Our

entry into Kathmandu was not perhaps very dignified, but at least it was light-hearted.

The pay-off of the Tempathang men, which was completed that afternoon (our farewells to our climbing Sherpas did not have to be made so soon), took place amid scenes probably unparalleled in Himalayan climbing history. The pay was handed out in a large room containing a ping-pong table. The Sherpas asked us to explain the use of this. We demonstrated, to their great delight, and soon found ourselves involved in a riotous game on the lines of progressive ping-pong, in which fourteen Sherpas took turns in swiping at the ball. They were so engrossed with this new toy that they could hardly be made to concentrate on receiving their pay, so that there was very little argument about it.

When it was time for them to go we were truly sorry, and I think they were too. Nima Lama, that good old man, took our hands in both of his, while tears stood in his eyes. There was no postal service to Tempathang, no way of ever sending a message to these friendly people. With our climbing Sherpas it was different—we could always write to them in Darjeeling, and the letter would eventually reach them, even in Sola Khombu; indeed, there had already been an exchange of addresses, and we hoped to climb with them again some day. With Murari it would of course be quite easy to keep in touch. But, unless by some miracle we were able to return to the Jugal Himal another year, our parting with our friends of Tempathang was final. While the pay-off was in progress the manager of the hotel came in with a photograph someone had taken of the three of us before we left for the mountains. The Sherpas pounced upon this and it was passed round from hand to hand amid exclamations of recognition. When it came to Tensing Lama's turn he pocketed the picture. " I'm keeping this," he said.

The Demon Chang

The manager protested that it was his property, but it was with some difficulty that he managed to get it back. " But, memsahib," cried Tensing Lama in an injured voice, " I want to nail it up in my house." " Can't you give *us* some pictures too? " asked other voices. We wished we could, but we had none to give. Later we congratulated each other. Dirty we may have appeared to be on our return to civilisation, ragged and thin, straight of hair and sunburnt of face—but by the lord we were pin-ups at last!

There are only a few things left to be said. We had not accomplished anything spectacular, but then we had never hoped to do so, with such a small party. We *had* succeeded in doing what we had set out to do, which was to reach and explore the Jugal Himal, the last large unexplored area of the Nepal Himalaya. That we had managed to climb an unknown peak of over 21,000 feet was really beside the point —a kind of bonus. We had been fortunate in that nothing at all had gone wrong, and that we had no illnesses or accidents. But it was not *all* luck; or, as Mark Twain is supposed to have said, " I find that the harder I work the luckier I am." We had worked extremely hard for nine months to plan and organise an efficient expedition. We had done so because we wanted our adventure to be a success, but in doing so we had proved that ordinary women can be as capable of carrying out such a project as men.

It was, by the way, just as well for us that we *were* successful. For, whereas a disaster in an all-male or mixed party may have passed almost unremarked and incurred nothing but sympathy, no mercy would have been shown to us if we had failed. The world was waiting to say " I told you so. What else can you expect of women? " Small wonder that we were determined to be well organised.

Of our time in the Jugal Himal we should like to say this. There is a belief current among mountaineers that while

Himalayan climbing is a great and unforgettable experience it is not as a rule fun, in the sense that climbing the Alps or among our own hills can be fun. The march to and from the mountains is reckoned to be far the most enjoyable part of Himalayan travel, while the climbing itself is said to be just a depressing grind which the climber endures as best he can so long as it gets him to the summit. With us this was certainly not the case. Much as we enjoyed parts of our march out and back, much as we loved Pomba Serebu, it was the days of strenuous endeavour we spent on the high ridges, glaciers and snowfields of the Jugal that will remain for ever in our memories as not only the happiest, but also, strangely enough, the most serene and peaceful days of our lives. Up there, each moment was sufficient for itself, and the world pressed upon us not at all.

THE END

For Those Who are Interested

FROM our position on the South ridge of Dorje Lakpa, looking west, we saw a series of glaciers which had receded until they had practically no ice-falls left, and now formed a comparatively flat ledge. This ledge started to the south of Dorje Lakpa and ran westward, to be joined by two big glaciers flowing between the mountains from the frontier ridge. It would not have been very difficult to reach from the cleft which had stopped us. This cleft dropped to a col which could easily be attained by climbing the ridge directly above a small frozen lochan situated below the crest of the ridge at about 17,000 feet, rather than keeping to the left of it as we had done. The western side of the col was a steep snow gully from the foot of which it would be quite possible to traverse to a point immediately beneath the start of the glacier ledge. To reach the ledge we saw that it would be necessary to climb some unpleasantly smooth and exposed slabs, but once over the *mauvais pas* it all looked to be plain sailing.

The most interesting result of Evelyn Camrass's expedition was that it proved the map wrong on a point that had puzzled us. According to the map two high ridges, descending from Phurbi Chyachu, lay between the Pulmutang and the Nosem Khola. We had felt pretty certain, from what we had seen on the way up, that there was only one, the ridge to which we had looked across from base camp.

This was the ridge Evelyn climbed, and from it she looked down into the Nosem Khola and across at the frontier ridge. The intermediate ridge and stream marked on the map did not in fact exist. We were able to confirm this later on when we saw the lie of the land from the shoulder of Chang Samaphu (13,000 feet), the highest point on the Nauling Lekh, on our way back to Kathmandu.

Of course, this was not the only time we proved the map to be inaccurate. For instance, the Nyakarkar, or Dorje Lakpa glacier, is marked as being longer and having a more gentle gradient than the Phurbi Chyachumbu, whereas in actual fact it is the other way round. The Dorje Lakpa glacier is far steeper and somewhat shorter. Then on the map the Phurbi Chyachumbu does not extend nearly so far north as the Nyakarkar. In reality it does, because the frontier ridge itself lies much farther north at this point than the map allows. The Ladies' Glacier, which is actually a steep arm, or tributary of the Phurbi Chyachumbu, and extends farther north than either of the two main glaciers, is not marked at all, though its proportions are considerable. There are several other minor errors, and the existence of two or three fine mountains is ignored. But on the whole the map does bear quite a close relation to the topography of the Jugal Himal, which is more than can be said of the maps of some of the other areas of the Nepal Himalaya.

APPENDIX: LIST OF MEDICAL STORES

Drugs

Penicillin, 1,000,000 units × 10
Sulphatriad G. ½ × 500
Sulphasuxidine G. ½ × 500
Phthalylsulphtahiazol G. ½ × 500
Terramycin 250 mgms. × 100
Penicillin lozenges × 40
Tyrosets × 144
Bradasol lozenges × 100
Chloramphenicol ear drops × 10 cc.
Albucid eye drops × ½ cc.
Pethidine 50 mgms. × 100
Codis tabs. × 300
Disprin tabs. × 300.
Codemprin tabs. × 200
Ophthalmic cocaine HCL 1/20 gr.
   1 tube
Sedonan ear drops × ½ fl. oz.
Morphia ¼ gr. × 20
   1 gr. × 20
   ½ gr. ampins. × 6
Abidec × 250
Ferrous sulphate, gr. 3, × 200
Vit. C tabs. × 200
Vit. B tabs × 100
Cascara sagrada gr. 2 × 100
Anusol suppositories × 12
Vegetable laxative tabs. × 20
Aludrox tabs × 500
Gelusil tabs. × 500
Castor oil capsules × 6
Dettol × 1 tin.
Iodine × 2 oz.
Pot. Permangate × 4 oz.
Orygen tabs. × 200
Sterile water for injection × 12 amps.
Surgical spirit, 16 fl. oz.
Dibistin × 100 tabs.
Benedryl caps. × 50
Caladryl cream × 8 fl. oz.
Vaseline × 2 oz.
Iodex × 2 tubes
Mylol insect repellant × 4 bottles
Sketofax × 5 tubes
Mycotic cream × 1 tube

Whitefields ointment × 2 oz.
D.D.T. with pyrethrum, 6 boxes
Wades abcess salve × 1 tube
Tannic acid jelly, 1 tube
Soneryl gr. 1½ × 100
Coramine, 6 amps containing ½ cc.
Paludrin tabs. × 500
Embaquin tabs. × 100
Ronicol × 100
Glycerine and thymol pastilles × 1 lb.
Glycerine and blackcurrent × 1 lb.
Zinc sulphate and adrenaline drops
   × ½ fl. oz.

First Aid Equipmemt

1 lb. cotton wool
2 gauze rolls
½ lb. white lint
3 triangular bandages
6 × 6 in. bandages
24 × 2 in. bandages
12 × 1 in. bandages
2 crepe bandages
4 Elastoplast bandages
6 tins of 6 in. P.O.P. bandages
Elastoplast strip dressings
2 viscopaste bandages
Jellonet burn dressings
Oiled silk
Sterile surgical sutures
Silkworm gut
Ethyl chloride spray

Medical Equipment

Stethescope
Scalpel and blades
Dental forceps
Artery forceps
Splinter forceps
Surgical scissors
Hypo syringes and needles
2 clinical thermometers
6 stitching needles

NOTE ON MEDICAL STORES

I HAVE listed on page 253 all the drugs, first-aid equipment and medical instruments which I took with me on the expedition. Most of these were supplied, free, by the various drug houses and instrument makers throughout Britain. Every manufacturer I wrote to met with my requests willingly, and most of them offered other drugs as well should I wish to include them.

It may be of interest to make a few comments on what I decided to take and what was actually required.

First I took the various symptoms, viz., pain, sleeplessness, sickness, and to these added infection and injury. This enabled me to think in terms of groups of drugs, for example—to cope with ascending degrees of pain I included increasingly active drugs such as those containing coedine, pethidine, and morphine. Next I thought of the body as a whole, and starting from the head I worked down to the feet considering each system separately, and what might go wrong with it.

My medical stores were certainly sufficient for us, as we were very fortunate to suffer no illness, accident or difficulty in sleeping. For Betty, Monica and myself I used in all only three soneryl tablets, about thirty coedine-like tablets, three Elastoplast bandages and a small quantity of antacid. I used paludrin and embaquin as prophylaxis against malaria and amoebic dysentry with complete success, and mylol and sketofax against the insects with some success. I did use quite a quantity of antacids, mild pain relievers and a smaller amount of the antibiotics to treat the local people who came seeking medical attention at each camp on the marches in and out.

Our own porters, carrying Sherpas and climbing Sherpas, also required some mild therapy. Many villagers came seeking help, especially for eye troubles, the most prevalent being cataract, tuberculous and venereal ulcers, and previous injuries which had left a scar on the cornea. All were complaining of degrees of blindness but unfortunately I could do little to help. I was unwilling to raise their hopes of cure by inserting harmless drops which I knew could have no beneficial effect. Where there was any superimposed infection I used suitable medication, I hope with some improvement in their sight.

I saw only three really ill people—an old man with dysentery, an old man with active pulmonary tuberculosis and a baby of two years old who had, I think, coeliac disease. Many others had headaches, stomach aches and skin sores. The headaches and stomach aches all seemed to respond to treatment, and I suspect that the novelty of receiving pills in brightly coloured wrappings from a strange white girl was the cause of many of the complaints. Contrary to my expectations very few of the villagers suffered from deficiency diseases except for goitre which was very prevalent. The people have a very mixed diet, utilising the wild plants as vegetables, growing grain and potatoes and rearing yacks and hens which give them milk, butter, cheese and eggs. They are small people but very strong.

The one thing I would like to have had with me and didn't was a large Winchester of cough mixture, to give to the people who had irritating coughs, due to the dust in the heat and the dryness in the cold of the glaciers. I think a few of the drugs could have been left out and a smaller quantity of others taken, but one must always err on the generous side, allowing a complete course of treatment for each member of the party against all likely diseases and enough to repeat the treatment at least once.

Both Betty and I had a short bout of food poisoning after returning to Kathmandu, due to eating bad meat, but we recovered quickly with no treatment other than starvation.

Our good health was due to several things—being well and fit when we left Britain, not eating or drinking anything on the train journeys except what our friends in Bombay and Delhi had given us and fruits with a removable skin, being absolutely insistent on all our water being boiled on the march below base camp, taking care not to tackle anything in the mountains which would have meant an unjustifiable risk, adequate food and clothing—and luck.

EVELYN M. McNICOL
(*formerly Camrass*)

About the Expedition Members

MONICA JACKSON was born in South India in 1920, and lived there, off and on, until 1953. She met and married her husband in Bangalore in 1942, and is now widowed. They had two children, both born in India. After graduating from Bennington College in Vermont, Jackson became a freelance journalist, eventually specialising in writing and lecturing on mountain travel and exploration. After her children grew up, she pursued graduate studies in social anthropology. Field research for these studies was earned out in rural South India, where Jackson lived sporadically for seven years in a mud and grain hut by the foot of the hills where she grew up. She is the author of *The Turkish Time Machine* (Hodder & Stoughton, 1966) and *Going Back* (Banyan Books, 1994). She lives in Edinburgh.

Following her trip to the Jugal Himal, ELIZABETH STARK made a traverse of the Cuillin Ridge in the Island of Skye with two friends from the Ladies' Scottish Climbing Club. The first all-women party to make this climb, they did it, in part, to celebrate the coronation of Elizabeth II of England and Elizabeth I of Scotland. Later, she moved to the United States to pursue graduate training in speech and language disorders. During this time, she traveled extensively in the United States and continued to climb, joining Evelyn on the Scottish Andean Expedition. In 1994, she retired from the Department of Audiology and Speech Sciences at Purdue University in West Lafayette, Indiana, where she continues to live. She and her husband have traveled to China, Indonesia and Australia. They plan to go to Thailand next year.

On returning from the expedition to the Jugal Himal, EVELYN CAMRASS married fellow climber Allan McNicol. She stopped her medical work for ten years while she raised three children. She was invited to join the Scottish Andean Expedition of 1964, which was a mixed expedition of eight men and two women, intending to climb Yerupaja, the second highest mountain in Peru. When she resumed her medical work, she became a consultant obstetrician and gynaecologist. She has kept up her climbing interest, making further trips to Peru, Nepal and Greenland. Now seventy-three, McNicol is looking forward to visiting Ladakh in July 2000 with the intent of joining other members of the Ladies' Scottish Climbing Club in an attempt to climb Stok Kangeri, a peak that measures above twenty thousand feet.

ARLENE BLUM is a writer, lecturer and mountaineer with a doctorate in biophysical chemistry. In her thirty years of climbing, she has taken part in more than twenty high-altitude expeditions, including the first all-woman climb of Mount McKinley and the 1976 American Bicentennial Expedition to Mount Everest. She is the author of *Annapurna: A Woman's Place,* an account of the first American ascent of Annapurna I. She lives in Berkeley, California, and presents lectures, leadership workshops and intercultural classes worldwide. For more information, visit www.arleneblum.com.

Titles from the Adventura Series

Climbing High: A Woman's Account of Surviving the Everest Tragedy, by Lene Gammelgaard. $25.00, 1-58005-023-9. The 1996 Everest disaster, recorded by a woman who made it to the summit and survived. An inspiring tale of one woman's spirit for adventure and a wholly original reflection on what it means to climb a mountain as dangerous and humbling as Everest.

Leading Out: Mountaineering Stories of Adventurous Women, edited by Rachel da Silva. $16.95, 1-58005-010-7. In more than twenty-five accounts by outstanding women climbers, this collection illustrates with eloquence and power how women are challenged and transformed by their experiences in the mountains.

No Mountain Too High: A Triumph Over Breast Cancer: The Story of the Women of Expedition Inspiration, by Andrea Gabbard. $16.00, 1-58005-008-5. This is the extraordinary story of seventeen women who battled breast cancer and then took on the challenge of climbing the Western Hemisphere's highest peak to raise public awareness about cancer.

The Curve of Time: The Classic Memoir of a Woman and Her Children Who Explored the Coastal Waters of the Pacific Northwest, by M. Wylie Blanchet. $14.95, 1-878067-27-3. The fascinating true adventure story of a woman who packed her five children into a twenty-five-foot boat and explored the coastal waters of the Pacific Northwest in the late 1920s.

Season of Adventure: Traveling Tales and Outdoor Journeys of Women Over 50, edited by Jean Gould. $15.95, 1-878067-81-8. Whether birdwatching in the Galápagos, camel-touring in Egypt or exploring the Pacific Cascades, these women display an uncommon *joie de vivre* and a keen awareness of their surroundings.

All the Powerful Invisible Things: A Sportswoman's Notebook, by Gretchen Legler. $12.95, 1-878067-69-9. Filled with a deep respect for wilderness, this beautifully written memoir traverses Legler's decade-long journey of self-discovery and reveals the ineffable grace of an outdoor life.

Another Wilderness: Notes from the New Outdoorswoman, edited by Susan Fox Rogers. $16.00, 1-878067-30-3. This collection of fresh and original writing by women cutting loose in the outdoors is sure to pull you from your armchair and send you off on adventures of your own.

Canyon Solitude: A Woman's Solo River Journey Through Grand Canyon, by Patricia C. McCairen. $14.95, 1-58005-007-7. A remarkable solo expedition down one of the world's most spectacular rivers.

Femme d'Adventure: Travel Tales from Inner Montana to Outer Mongolia, by Jessica Maxwell. $14.00, 1-878067-98-2. Maxwell recounts tales of trailing humpback whales, braving whitewater rapids, catching a glimpse of tropical manatees, chasing wild mustangs and trotting the globe from Ireland to Venice and beyond.

Gifts of the Wild: A Woman's Book of Adventure, from the Editors of Adventura Books. $16.95, 1-58005-006-9. From the spectacular mountains of Patagonia to the mossy woods of the Pacific Northwest, *Gifts of the Wild* explores the transformative power of outdoor adventure in the lives of women.

Solo: On Her Own Adventure, edited by Susan Fox Rogers. $12.95, 1-878067-74-5. Whether they light out for a day hike in the Adirondacks, bodyboard with dolphins off the California coast, pedal across New Zealand or road trip through the northwestern United States, each contributor to *Solo* describes the inspiring challenges and exhilarating rewards of going it alone.

Uncommon Waters: Women Write About Fishing, edited by Holly Morris. $16.95, 1-878067-76-1. An anthology that captures the bracing adventure and meditative moments of fishing in the words of thirty-four women anglers.

Rivers Running Free: A Century of Women's Canoeing Adventures, edited by Judith Niemi and Barbara Wieser. $16.95, 1-878067-90-7. Embarking on both wilderness expeditions and trips through the urban wilds, these women eloquently record the influence canoeing has had on their lives and the boundaries it has inspired them to push beyond.

SEAL PRESS publishes many books of fiction and nonfiction by women writers. If you are unable to obtain a Seal Press title from a bookstore or would like a free catalog of our books, please order from us directly by calling 800-754-0271. Visit our website at www.sealpress.com.